FINANCIAL FACTORS AND CORPORATE INVESTMENT

To My Parents

Financial Factors and Corporate Investment

An empirical analysis of Korean manufacturing firms

YONG-DOO CHO

Avebury

Aldershot • Brookfield USA • Hong Kong • Singapore • Sydney

Published by
Avebury
Ashgate Publishing Limited
Gower House
Croft Road
Aldershot
Hants GU11 3HR
England

Ashgate Publishing Company
Old Post Road
Brookfield
Vermont 05036
USA

British Library Cataloguing in Publication Data

Cho, Yong-Doo
Financial factors and corporate investment
1. Investments – Korea 2. Corporations, Korean – Finance
I. Title
658.1'5'09519

ISBN 1 85972 366 7

Library of Congress Catalog Card Number: 95-83843

Printed and bound by Athenaeum Press, Ltd.,
Gateshead, Tyne & Wear.

Contents

List of tables and figures

List of abbreviations

GAAP	Generally Accepted Accounting Principles
GMM	General Method of Moments
KIS	Korea Investors Service
KSE	Korea Stock Exchange
KSIC	Korea Standard Industry Code
NBFI	Non-Bank Financial Institution
OLS	Ordinary Least Square
SNA	Standard National Accounting

Acknowledgements

This monograph is a revised version of my D.Phil. thesis at the University of Oxford, completed in May 1995.

The outcome of this research would have been much less satisfactory without the support of many individuals and organisations. First of all, I owe a special debt to my supervisor Stephen Bond in conducting this research. I have benefited greatly from his encouragement and suggestions at every stage, although any remaining shortcomings of the thesis belong to me. Discussions with Sonia Bhalotra, Christopher Bliss, Jennifer Corbett, and Hyunsong Shin are also gratefully acknowledged. Colin Mayer and Michael Devereux, who kindly served as the examiners of my D.Phil. thesis, provided me with invaluable comments, some of which I could not fully incorporate into this book. Data provided by Korea Investors Service in the early stage was crucial to the progress of the research and I am very grateful for their generosity. Professional advice on the interpretation of Korean company accounts from Sanghyuck Park and Bonghan Yoon of Arthur Anderson and KPMG in London, respectively, was also very useful.

It is important to stress that this work was only made possible thanks to the benevolent financial support of the POSCO Scholarship Society. The George-Webb Medley fund at the Social Studies faculty in Oxford and MacKinnon Travel funds at Magdalen College, Oxford, were also very helpful in financing my research trip to Korea. In the stage of preparing for a final manuscript for this book, I greatly benefited from congenial atmosphere of the School of East Asian Studies at Sheffield and especially encouragement from Ian Gow, Chairman of the Department.

Last but not least, my dearest thanks go to my family. I cannot find suitable words to thank my wife Kyungjin, who has shared the ups and downs of my research during our life at Oxford. Our two childeren, Hyunjung and Seunghan, were always a joy which provided the source of our energies and I dedicate this book to them.

1 Introduction

The aim of this monograph is to investigate the impact of financial factors on corporate investment in Korea, principally using firm-level company accounts data. The focus of our research is on whether investment spending is constrained by the availability of finance and whether some types of firms are more affected by financial constraints than others.

Korea provides an interesting case study in that there were very high rates of investment in the last three decades of economic development, and the history of government intervention in the allocation of investment finance has resulted in different types of firms facing different conditions in financial markets. Heterogeneity in the access of firms to investment finance is likely to be more important in Korea than in most developed countries. During the 1980s financial liberalisation has brought about important changes in the Korean financial system, although the effects of these reforms remains controversial. We are particularly interested in whether the investment spending of firms that are affiliated to 'Chaebol' industrial groups and other large firms is affected differently by financial constraints from the investment of non-group affiliated firms and smaller firms.

There already exists substantial evidence from developed countries such as the UK, US and Japan indicating that investment spending can be affected by financial constraints, even in developed financial systems and for large quoted companies (e.g. Fazzari, Hubbard and Petersen 1988), Hayashi and Inoue 1991, Devereux and Schiantarelli 1990, Blundell, Bond, Devereux and Schiantarelli 1992). There is also evidence that firms with different characteristics such as financial policies or group affiliation are affected differently (e.g. Hoshi, Kashyap and Scharfstein 1991, Devereux and Schiantarelli 1990, Bond and Meghir 1994a).

In contrast, much less evidence exists for companies in developing countries. We are aware of only three similar studies using microeconomic data for Korea (Kong 1992, Atiyas 1992, Chen and Chowdhury 1992), all of which report results only for the Q model of investment. We will estimate a broader range of econometric investment models, including accelerator-type models and Euler equation models as well as the Q model. We have also collected a larger sample of company accounts data covering a longer time period than these previous studies, and use what we consider to be more appropriate econometric methods.

For this analysis, we use company accounts data for an unbalanced panel of 367 large manufacturing corporations over the period 1982-1991. These firms were quoted on the Korea Stock Exchange by the end of 1991. The company accounts data provides information on investment, cash flow, sales and sources of finance that can be used to investigate these issues. We also matched this company accounts data to stock market valuations for these firms to allow the construction of measures of Tobin's Q. Before we embark on econometric testing, we investigate the patterns of investment finance of Korea corporate sector, using both aggregate data and firm-level data.

The outline of the remainder of the book is as follows.

Chapter 2 reviews the structure of the Korean financial system and the key developments over the last three decades, highlighting the importance of government intervention in the allocation of investment finance over this period. Especially in the 1960s and 1970s government financial policy played a subordinate role to government industrial policy, which systematically favoured certain types of firms, namely large firms and firms affiliated to 'Chaebol' industrial groups. The distinctive features of these Korean 'Chaebol' groups are also explained in Chapter 2. We emphasize that the result of this policy was a differential cost and/or access to investment finance, which is likely to have resulted both in different patterns of investment finance for different types of corporation, and a differential impact of financial constraints on investment spending. This chapter also explains how although the 1980s was characterised by financial liberalisation and a gradual withdrawal of government intervention in the financial system, these advantages for large and 'Chaebol' group affiliated firms have tended to persist.

In Chapter 3 we investigate the pattern of investment finance for Korean companies using aggregate data sources, both from sectoral National Accounts and from aggregated company accounts data published by the Bank of Korea for a representative sample of manufacturing firms. Following the methodology developed by Mayer (1988), we show that Korean corporations have used a very low share of investment finance from internal funds by comparison with other major economies; and correspondingly high shares of finance from bank loans and in the late 1980s from securities markets, due to the rapid growth of the Korean stock market and bond market which resulted from the policy of financial liberalisation.

In Chapter 4 we perform a similar analysis using individual accounts data for a balanced sample of 420 large corporations (quoted by the end of 1991) over the period 1983-1991. This data was collected from Korea Investors Service for analysis in this book. The advantage of using individual company accounts in Chapter 4 is that it allows us to investigate differences between Chaebol affiliated firms and non-Chaebol firms, as well as between larger and smaller quoted corporations. Using a similar methodology to that used in Chapter 3, we indeed find that there were significant differences in the pattern of investment finance between these different types of firms. These differences are generally in line with predictions from prior knowledge as outlined in Chapter 2.

Chapter 5 presents a review of recent econometric research on testing for the impact of financial constraints on company investment spending.

Interest in this question was revived during the 1980s by both theoretical developments and by results from microeconometric studies of investment. We also consider how the hierarchy of finance model predicts a differential impact of financial constraints on favoured and unfavoured firms in the Korean context. We survey previous findings from similar studies using company accounts data for both the major developed countries and for developing countries.

In Chapter 6 we present our microeconometric study of the relation between corporate investment and financial constraints using company accounts for large Korean corporations. We estimate an eclectic range of econometric investment models, including traditional accelerator-type specifications as well as structural dynamic models like the Q and Euler equation models. General Method of Moments estimators are used to allow for unobserved firm-specific effects and for the endogeneity of explanatory variables. In addition to estimating these investment models for our total sample, we also consider sub-samples of the data based on group-affiliation and size, as well as on age, export propensity and industry sector. Our main findings suggest that there is evidence of financial constraints affecting investment spending by firms in Korea, and that this evidence does appear to be concentrated among smaller and non-Chaebol affiliated corporations. This evidence suggests that larger firms and Chaebol group affiliated firms continued to enjoy financial advantages in the 1980s. Our results are compared to a similar study using Japanese company data (Hoshi, Kashyap and Scharfstein 1991), although we emphasize that the structure of Korean Chaebol groups is quite different from the structure of Japanese Keiretsu groups.

2 The structure of investment finance in Korea

2.1 Introduction

In this chapter, we will describe the main features of the Korean financial system and how government policy has affected the evolution of the financial system in Korea. In this discussion, the main focus will be on how the corporate sector has financed its investment spending in the changing environment of the Korean financial system since 1960. Although we will cover the last three decades, we are particularly interested in the 1980s since the data we analyse in this book relates mostly to that period. This chapter is intended to provide some background understanding of the Korean financial system. In later chapters we investigate the pattern of investment finance in the Korean corporate sector, using aggregate and company accounts flow of funds data in Chapters 3 and 4 respectively; and investigate the impact of financial constraints on corporate investment in Korea using an econometric analysis of company accounts data in Chapter 6.

Until recently, academic interest in the Korean financial system was centred around the effects of financial repression and whether this should be reduced. The proponents of financial liberalization argued that the repressed financial system should be replaced by a more market-oriented financial system, with less government intervention. The bottom line of their argument is that government failure is greater than market failure. However, in the light of the experience of some successful developing countries including Korea, the recent literature in contrast emphasizes the benefits of selective and consistent government intervention in the financial system, even if they recognise the potential harmful effects of having an inefficient financial system. Cho (1989), in discussing the Korean experience, argued that 'the shape of the financial system, the way risky investments are financed, and the way financial arrangements affect the incentive structure of firms may be no less important factors that account for the success of economic growth'. They at least point out that at certain stages of development some countries might need careful coordination by the government between the financial sector and the real sector (see World Bank 1993).

However, it is important to note that this chapter will not address these big questions on the roles of the financial system and government intervention, but will simply describe as clearly as possible the structure of the Korean financial system at each stage of its development, and especially in the 1980s.

In the next section, we briefly describe the main components of the Korean financial system and the main developments during the period since 1960. Having described the structure of the financial system, we look separately at two sub-periods, the 1960s and 1970s, and the 1980s. In the third section, we discuss how the Korean government's industrial policy affected its financial policy and therefore the development of the financial system by examining the relationships between government, business and banks. Finally we describe the resulting Korean industrial and financial structure that has emerged from this experience, with particular reference to the role of 'Chaebol' industrial groups which will play an important role in our subsequent analysis.

2.2 The Korean financial system

It is difficult to characterise the Korean financial system in short because it has evolved considerably during the last three decades, although it has certainly maintained some common features. Finance in Korea has been consistently repressed and manipulated by the government, and market segmentation has been prevalent, of course to varying degrees at different times. We start by describing some general features of the system especially in the period before the 1980s, and then move our focus onto the main structural changes in the 1980s.

Up to the end of the 1950s, the Korean financial system was severely underdeveloped and the basic structure had been inherited from the period of Japanese domination (1919-1945). It was only in the early 1960s, when the military regime led by Park, Chung-Hee formed the government in 1961 and started the new economic development plan in 1963, that the financial system began to undergo substantial changes. During the period 1948-1961, the financial system suffered from an extreme shortage of funds. The then government, pursuing an import-substitution policy, provided special funds to certain privileged importers, which were mainly large firms with strong political connections.[1] The source of these funds was mostly reconstruction-related foreign aid.

Overview of financial sector

In Korea, the financial system can be characterised as a dual structure where formal sector coexist with informal sector.[2] The formal sector consists of the Bank of Korea[3] and other banking institutions, non-bank financial institutions and the securities market. The informal sector is conveniently called 'curb' market.

The formal financial sector broadly consists of the banking institutions and non-bank financial intermediaries (NBFI). The former includes the Bank of Korea, nationwide commercial banks, local banks and some special banks. The Korean banking sector, which dates back to the Japanese domination period, has been tightly controlled by the government, which owned the majority of shares in the nationwide commercial banks from 1961 to 1983. Several special banks were established by the government, each under a special law in the 1960s.

But in reality, contrary to their original purpose, they had to compete for deposits from the general public, rather than receiving significant government funds.

Some NBFIs were added to the financial sector just after the Presidential emergency decree in 1972.[4] The purpose of those institutions was to channel funds in the informal sector to the formal financial sector. Investment and finance, mutual savings and finance companies and credit unions were included in this category and prospered remarkably in the 1970s.

The securities market in Korea consists of the equity market and the bond market. There is also the money market which intermediates between the short-term demand for and supply of funds of various economic entities. In Korea, the money market embraces the call market and a wide range of other financial markets including those for Treasury Bills, Monetary Stabilization Bonds, negotiable certificates of deposits, repurchase agreements and commercial paper.

The informal financial sector, or so-called 'curb' market, is a large, well organized system of credit brokers and dealers. The sources of funds in this market are heterogeneous, but the uses are now principally for the working capital of large firms and small and medium-sized firms. The average interest rates on curb loans are much higher than those for loans in the regulated market, but different interest rates are charged for different borrowers using a sophisticated credit rating system; blue chip companies pay substantially lower interest rates than less reputable borrowers. Most of these loans do not require the use of collateral, which indicates that the risk of default is accounted for in the interest rates charged.

The interest rate on the curb market is regularly surveyed by the Bank of Korea (see Table 2.2) but the size of the market[5] is relatively unknown. The most official and reliable information on the size of the market comes from the sum of curb market borrowings declared by business firms under the 1972 Presidential emergency decree. By this decree, all enterprises with a business licence were required to report their informal borrowings. The total of outstanding informal debt declared by firms amounted to 345.6 billion won, equivalent to 80 % of the then money supply (M1), while the formal debt of business sector was 1239.8 billion won in total.

Financial repression in the 1960s and 1970s

At the time the military regime took power in 1961, the financial system in Korea was seriously underdeveloped and segmented. The corporate sector, being short of finance from the formal sector, had to rely mostly on the curb market and on foreign assistance. In 1961, the government confiscated shares in commercial banks which had previously been owned by the then Chaebol groups and furthermore the share ownership of any individual shareholder was restricted to 10 % of the total votes. In this way the government effectively took control of the commercial banks.

In 1965, the government initiated a major reform of interest rates, which almost doubled official interest rates on time deposits in the commercial banks (see Table 2.2). The banks' loan rates were also raised, although the increase of the rates was not applied to the low subsidy loan rate for some favoured strategic firms and sectors. The main aim of this policy was to stimulate the growth of financial system and, through this, to contribute to the growth of the economy.[6] As reported in Table 2.1, the ratio of the money supply (M2) to GNP showed a dramatic increase between 1965 and 1970.

Notwithstanding the increase in the savings rate during the latter half of the 1960s (see Table 2.1), the policy turned out to be short-lived. By the beginning of the 1970s, the government turned back to a low interest rate policy, following a rethink of economic development strategy. Until then, the main strategy was that, using the relatively cheap labour costs in Korea compared to other developing countries, the government encouraged and gave incentives to firms which produced labor-intensive goods for export, by providing them with cheap loans. But in the early 1970s a consensus emerged that due to the changing economic environment, the economy needed to move from labour-intensive manufacturing industries to heavy and chemical industries.[7] However, there was still a great shortage of loanable funds in the financial system, while this project required high levels of capital investment. The government chose to control the financial sector, especially the banking system, more tightly than before, rather than to foster the growth of the financial sector by continuing the interest rate reform begun in 1965. In the 1970s, the financial system was perhaps more repressed by the government than at any other time in the last three decades. The government went back to a low interest rate policy in the early 1970s and kept the real interest rate for general bank loans around zero, as we see in Table 2.2.[8] If we take into account the interest rates on preferential loans, the average real interest rate on bank loans in the 1970s must have been significantly negative. The growth of the financial sector stagnated in the 1970s. As reported in Table 2.1, the M2 to GNP ratio even dropped from 35 % in 1970 to 31.3 % in 1975.

To transfer funds from the curb market to the formal sector, the government introduced two important measures. First, in 1972, the government declared the Presidential emergency decree under which enterprises with a business licence were required to report their informal borrrowings.[9] Second, in 1973 the government introduced the Acts under which some non-bank financial intermediaries such as investment and finance companies were established to attract funds from the informal sector to the formal sector. These NBFIs grew very quickly in the 1970s, since the government regulation of these institutions was weaker than that covering banks, and therefore they could pay and earn somewhat higher interest rates.

New developments in the 1980s

At the end of the 1970s, it seemed evident that the big investment in heavy and chemical industries in the 1970s had resulted in substantial excess capacity, and non-performing loans were increasing in the banking sector. More importantly, the view emerged that the government's highly inter-ventionist policy was responsible for this imbalance in the economy, and that the Korean economy had become too complex for government officials to manage. Partly in reaction to this opinion, the government made a commitment to increase the role of market mechanisms in economic policy-making.

Other than these domestic causes, there were also external causes for adopting the financial liberalisation policy. From the late 1970s, the Korean government came under pressure from the US government to open not only the real sector but also the financial sector to international competition. The US government required its Korean counterpart to allow foreign banks to establish branches and foreign investors to invest in the Korean equity market without any restriction by the end of the 1980s at the latest.[10] All this pressure was included as part of the package of market opening pressure directed at Japan and some other highly developing countries which had long-term trade imbalances with the US.

The 1980s saw many changes in the Korean financial system since the government launched the financial reform program. While the effectiveness of these financial reforms is arguable, it is widely agreed that the process of reforming the financial system was rather gradual. The government has introduced some changes and these measures and effects can be summarised as follows.

The redirection of financial policy formally started with the sale of shares in the large commercial banks between 1981 and 1983.[11] Although commercial banks were privatised, the process of liberation was seriously constrained by the accumulated non-performing loans in the banks. Instead of fully liberalizing the banking sector, the government introduced more flexibility in interest rate decisions of NBFIs. Indeed, in Table 2.1 we observe a consistently declining share of total deposits in the banks and the opposite trend for the share of total deposit in the NBFIs in the 1980s.

Second, as the inflation rate dropped sharply from 1982, as shown in Table 2.2, the real interest rate rose to a high positive level, which meant that the corporate sector became more burdened with interest costs. The government reacted to this by reducing nominal interest rates, but that measure was not very effective because the inflation rate fell ever faster. The high real interest rate contributed to the rapid growth of the financial sector, especially non-bank financial intermediaries as they were allowed to offer higher interest rates than the banks. The government did not free the movement of bank interest rates until 1991.

Third, the promotion of the securities market was both necessary and inevitable for the Korean economy. As the government introduced more liberalising measures into the financial system, it could not rely any more on the banking system to provide cheap finance to selected industries, particularly because the banking sector was burdened with non-performing loans. It was expected that the stock market would provide both attractive outlets for savers and cheap finance for investors.[12] The pressure from the US to open Korean financial markets also made it inevitable to develop the stock market.

The number of companies listed on the Korean Stock Exchange rose from 342 in 1985 to 669 at the end of 1990 and the total market value of listed stocks increased from 6 trillion won in 1985 to 79 trillion won in 1990, as shown in Table 2.3. Along with the development of the stock market, the bond market has expanded rapidly in the 1980s. Total issues of corporate bonds has more than tripled in the 1980s.[13]

The role of direct government intervention in the allocation of investment finance to selected firms and sectors has greatly diminished in the course of the 1980s. Up to about 1983 the government continued to support firms that were in financial distress as a result of its previous policy. Even this support diminished after 1983. However, the process of financial liberalisation was hampered by structural factors such as the weak corporate financial structure, and fragile banking sector burdened with non-performing loans and competition with NBFIs, and therefore the pace of financial liberalisation tended to be rather slow.

2.3 Industrial policy and the relationships between government, business and banks

In the previous section, we reviewed the historical development of the Korean financial system. But it is important to point out that the Korean financial system has been shaped by the course of industrial policy. Especially in the 1960s and 1970s, the government's financial policy was basically to ensure that sufficient financial resources could be provided to the sectors and firms that were favoured by the government's industrial policy.

The military government that was formed in 1961 introduced a series of 5-year economic development plans, starting in 1963. The military government redirected industrial policy from import-substitution to an export-led strategy. Although the focus of the policy evolved during the 1960s and 1970s, financial repression was used throughout as a crucial tool for achieving the industrial targets.

In the early 1960s there were many stumbling blocks to this export-led economic policy. First of all the number and quality of entrepreneurs were inadequate and Korean industrialists did not have sufficient knowledge of foreign markets and international marketing. Even if there were suitable candidate for export activities, financing these projects was a major problem since the Korean economy was suffering from a low savings rate and chronic current account deficits.

The solution adopted by the government was to intervene in every aspect of business activity. It could not wait for the financial system to develop efficiently. The government itself selected the sectors or companies to lead the Korean export drive according to its own criteria. It did not give opportunities to all firms on an equal footing, but rather favoured the established large firms. Many of these were member companies of 'Chaebol' groups, which means a group of firms centred around a holding company and effectively controlled by the founding family. These Chaebol groups had mostly established themselves just after the Korean War, and prospered during the import-substitution period.

In the early 1960s, many of the currently active Chaebol companies were already established in business. The military government introduced legislation under which the assets of leading businessmen were confiscated if they were considered to have accumulated their wealth by abusing positions of power and influence. It took control of financial flows by seizing the majority of shares in the commercial banks from these Chaebol groups. It intervened in every activity of these commercial banks, from appointing the chairman and executives to decision on individual loans decision-making. The monetary policy of the Bank of Korea was totally controlled by the Ministry of Finance. It also tightly controlled capital inflows and outflows to fix the exchange rate and, by doing so, it could also regulate nominal interest rates. As the export-oriented development strategy was established, the government urged these Chaebol firms and other large firms to play an active role in economic growth. The basic government strategy in this period was to expand the economy by increasing the volume of exports, whilst protecting the domestic real and financial markets.

Once selected by the government as 'strategic', the favoured sectors or firms could benefit from foreign loans and loans from commercial banks on the favourable terms.[14] In the case of foreign loans, the source could be either foreign governments or foreign commercial banks. As the borrowing from foreign sources was guaranteed by the Korea Development Bank and Economic Planning Board, in the event of the default, the risk of not being paid was minimised. This foreign loan guarantee system has sharply increased the amount of foreign loan in the course of 1960s.[15]

In the 1970s, without discouraging export industries, the government turned its attention to building up heavy and chemical industries.[16] In view of the fact that most of successful existing industries were light industries, this development of heavy and chemical industries posed a formidable burden for Korean corporations. Most companies regarded this investment as unprofitable in the short-term and requiring too long a payback period. These projects did not appear commercially attractive.

The government again provided low-cost long-term finance to firms undertaking this investment through the banking sector.

This practice in the 1960s and 1970s was possible because the government was controlling the main flows of finance; it tightly controlled the commercial banks, by owning the majority of shares of those banks. The gamut of intervention in the banking system varied from setting ceilings for lending and borrowing interest rates to appropriating loanable funds for specific industries or firms. The government also created new financial institutions to accommodate the needs of the industrial sector. In the 1960s, new special banks were added to the system mainly to support the export industries. After 1972, when the Presidential Decree was declared to freeze the corporate debt from the 'curb' market, non-bank financial intermediaries such as investment and finance companies and investment trust companies were introduced.

All in all, the 1960s and 1970s can be characterised as a period in which the financial sector played only a passive role, in that it was used to facilitate the government's industrial policy in the real sector.

Embedded in the Korean financial system in the 1960s and 1970s described above is a close and interactive triangular relationship between three players: government, business and banking sector.

The government maintained a close relationship with industry through various formal and informal channels. Government officials and the heads of favoured firms often met and discussed the firms' investment plans of the firms. Once selected as capable entrepreneurs for strategic investment projects, these firms were duly provided with the necessary risk capital for the required investment. If such firms got into financial distress, the government organised rescue plans in conjunction with commercial banks. In this way, for example, the government was able to provide these firms with sufficient incentives to invest in heavy and chemical industries in the 1970s. This mechanism consequently brought about an intimate relationship between the government and firms in the priority business sector.

This arrangement was attractive to the industrial firms because they could concentrate on the expansion of their output and exports, rather than worrying about their immediate profitability, as the government itself put more emphasis on expanding the size of the economy than on producing high short-term returns from particular projects. In short, the active role of the government as an effective risk partner made it possible for selected Korean firms and sectors to take a longer-term view of their business and investment decisions (see Cho and Cole 1986 and Cho, 1989).

In this process, the banks did not play an active role in assessing and monitoring investment projects. Most lending decisions were taken by government officials, and the banking sector only had to implement their decisions. This process later resulted in an accumulation of bad debts from the policy loans.

This subordinate role for banks was a peculiar part of the Korean financial system in the 1960s and 1970s. Zysman (1983) called it a 'state-controlled' bank-based system. In Korea, the proportion of investment financed from bank lending was traditionally high, but this should not be interpreted as a sign that the Korean banks were performing a delegated monitoring function properly. It was rather possible because the government supported these lending decisions with a guarantee that if there was any default in repayment, the government would bail out the troubled firms.

A commercial bank, before making most of its loans to individual borrowers, would first approach the Bank of Korea to ascertain whether or not it would discount or make loans against the credit documents that the commercial bank would receive from its borrowers in return for the loans. The Bank of Korea then consulted the government for approval of the loan.If the government approved then the commercial bank went ahead and made the loan. In effect, the government lent directly to the borrower, with the commercial bank and the Bank of Korea being little more than intermediaries in the process.

This Korean-style bank-based financial system should be distinguished from the more typical bank-based financial systems, such as we observe in Germany and Japan. In Germany and Japan, the long-term relationships between firms and banks are often based on economic incentives, through such methods as equity participations, and the banks play a delegated monitoring function. This is rendered possible by the bank sharing the risks faced by the firm (Mayer 1988). It can be said that in Korea the government acted as the risk sharer, like the banks in Germany and Japan, even if Korean banks did not have equity participation in industrial firms. By owning the banks and directing their loans, the government became an active risk partner of the favoured firms. By pushing banks to lend to the chosen firms at controlled interest rates and sharing the risk of the investment, it increased the expected return of the investment to these firms.

By the end of 1970s, it was evident that there had been a substantial increase in the share of total investment accounted for by heavy and chemical industries and that this was caused by the government's distorted intervention in the financial system. A consensus emerged that the share of investment in the heavy and chemical industries was too high, and that further investment would be misallocation of capital. The negative impacts of this close government-business-bank relationship can therefore be summarised as follows.

First, financial intervention led to excessive economic concentration and resource misallocation. Firms which could borrow at the controlled interest rate grew bigger and bigger, favoured by the government in financial aspects as well as in other aspects of policy. Even when these firms were in financial distress, they expected that the government would bail them out through the banking system. This was partly a political decision as a run of bankruptcies among the big industrial firms would essentially mean the failure of the Korean economy. In contrast, small and medium-sized firms and other unfavoured firms found it difficult to secure long-term finance even at a high cost of capital. They often had to rely on short-term borrowing from the 'curb' market at excessively high interest rates.

Secondly, this practice slowed the growth of the financial sector. The government-owned banks eventually became unprofitable because they had to follow the instructions of the government. By the beginning of the 1980s, overinvestment in the heavy and chemical industries had left these banks with considerable non-performing loans. Again, these unprofitable banks could be sustained only by the support of the risk assuming government.

Thirdly, this practice left the favoured firms and sectors with very high debt-equity ratios. Debt-equity ratios for Korean firms tend to be high in comparison with those for firms in most developed countries, as well as in the NICs (see Kim 1990). This feature left Korean firms more vulnerable to external shocks or to changes in the macroeconomic environment than those of other countries. For example, the financial viability of Korean firms is threatened whenever interest rates rise or the credit supply is reduced by amounts that would be considered quite manageable in other countries. This debt overhang constrained monetary policy and the process of financial liberalization in the 1980s (see World Bank 1989).

The 1980s can be characterised as the period in which the government tried to become less involved in this triangular relationship and the bank-firm relationships began to be based more on economic reasons than on policy considerations. Coupled with the aftermath of the second oil shock and the political instability caused by the assassination of the late President, Park Chung-Hee, criticism mounted concerning the possible harmful impacts of heavy government intervention during the 1970s, and a series of financial reforms were introduced by the government, as we have noted in section 2.2 However, the process of financial reform in the 1980s was very gradual for the following reasons.

First, the high debt ratio of the corporate sector made it very vulnerable to external shocks and economic fluctuations, and required even more government involvement in banks' credit allocation to bail out troubled firms and industries at the start of the 1980s (see Cho and Cole 1986). The government has since attempted to reduce the debt ratio by assigning a 'main bank' to each Chaebol group and requiring this bank to monitor and control the amount of credit extended.

Second, the banking sector was itself vulnerable, partly because of the high level of bad debt accumulated during the heavy and chemical industry drive in the 1970s, and partly because of competition with the less regulated NBFIs. The banks continued to be reliant on the government to obtain some emergency funds.

Third, Chaebol groups have grown into powerful business groups and they have sought to protect their interests by opposing the government reform policy. This opposition became more pronounced in the latter half of the 1980s.

More recently there has also been more emphasis placed on the possible beneficial effects of government intervention in financial markets. According to orthodox proponents of financial liberalization, the financial system should not have been repressed and economic growth in Korea was either not related to this financial repression or was achieved in spite of it. Two new approaches have sought to qualify or revise this orthodoxy.

First, there are views that regard the government-business-bank relationship in terms of an internal organisation framework, a concept similar to the idea of 'organisational hierarchy' developed by Williamson (1975). Lee (1992) described the Korean relationship as quasi-internal organisation; Cho and Hellman (1993) used the term 'Government-led internal organisation' (GLIO) for the 1960s and 1970s and 'Private-sector led internal organisation' (PLIO) for the 1980s. The idea of this approach is that in Korea, the triangular relationship has operated as a *de facto* internal capital market. Through the close cooperation and long-term relationship among the government, business and banks, the state-controlled bank-based system allows 'lender monitoring' to be carried out efficiently in the sense that transaction costs were minimised. Lee (1992) also argued that as the economy developed and became more complex, as in Korea in the 1980s, the benefits of these quasi-internal organisation institutions diminished and the problems of organisational failure became more serious.

A second line of argument, broadly attacking the orthodox proponents of financial liberalisation, considers how the institutional and political framework of East Asian NICs may have contributed to the rapid economic growth of these countries. Most of these approaches emphasize the interactive relationship between government and business, and the market-conforming approach taken by the government. Amsden (1989) and Amsden and Euh (1993) argued that the Korean industrial strategy was effective because it was strongly backed up by the repressive financial policy, even suggesting that financial repression is an essential feature of 'late industrialisation'.[17] Wade (1988,1989) emphasized the importance of the role of the government as a provider of long-term finance in Korea in the 1960s and 1970s, and further argued that a credit-based system could be a better option for developing countries than a stock-market based system. Stiglitz (1989) also stressed that capital markets in developing countries are more severely affected by the problem of asymmetric information, and also handicapped by weak regulatory frameworks. In these circumstances he suggested that promoting capital markets at the expense of the banking sector could be harmful.

2.4 Korean industrial structure and corporate financing behaviour

Korean industrial policy, favouring the export-oriented industries and firms and the heavy and chemical industries in the 1960s and 1970s, has resulted in a distinctive industrial structure in Korea. This was called a 'dual' structure by Lee (1992); there is a relatively small number of large firms, most of which belong to Chaebol groups, and a relatively large number of small and medium-sized firms. Table 2.4 shows the Chaebols' dominant share of activity in the manufacturing sector. For the top five Chaebols, the share of manufacturing sales increased from 15.7 % in 1978 to 23.0 % in 1985. As we have discussed, the government consistently favoured certain sectors and firms which conformed to the Economic Development Plans. These firms typically belonged to Chaebol groups. Even if they did not initially belong to one of these groups, they were mostly large firms and eventually developed into Chaebol groups themselves. This is one of the most salient features of the Korean corporate sector in the 1980s.

Most Chaebol groups were founded as relatively modest organisations by an individual or a family, mostly in the 1950s after the Korean War, although some date back as far as the late 19th century or early 20th century. These groups enjoyed spectacular growth in the 1960s and 1970s, largely owing to government intervention. The five largest Chaebol groups, Samsung, Hyundai, Daewoo, Lucky-Goldstar, and Sunkyung, are all listed among the Fortune 500 largest industrials outside the United States in 1990 (see Lee 1990). These conglomerates have a number of typical features, which we describe below.

First, most Chaebols are still effectively controlled by the founder-family. They maintain control over the group through a combination of interlocking directorates and cross-holdings of stocks among the affiliated firms. The founder-family usually owns about 10-20 % of the total outstanding shares of the group's companies as a whole.

Second, the Chaebol groups are forbidden from controlling commercial banks. Although some Chaebols have in-house financial companies such as insurance companies, securities companies and provincial banks, the groups are not allowed to own more than 8 % of the shares of major commercial banks. The main worry is that if Chaebol groups were allowed to own commercial banks, economic concentration would be further increased as the Chaebol group would direct subsidised loans to affiliated companies.

Third, most Chaebol groups are built around a flagship company, called the General Trading Company. Since 1975 the government has designated certain firms as 'general trading companies' and granted them favourable treatment in international bidding, loosened restrictions on their importation of raw materials, and provided funds for the stockpiling of finished export goods (Choi 1993). In most Chaebol groups, General Trading Company functions as the coordinator of group's export activities. As the benefits of General Trading Company status were considerable, it was important to renew this status every year, which depended on past export performance. To some extent these advantages in international trade granted to general trading companies have continued to operate up to the present day, although their importance was reduced in the 1980s.

Fourth, each group has very diverse areas of business.[18] As we discussed in section 2.3, the Chaebols followed the strategy of diversifying their business areas to benefit from the changes in the emphasis of the government's industrial policy. For example, most Chaebol companies entered into the heavy and chemical industries in the mid-1970s. If a business group was only engaged in a single line of business, it would run the risk of a credit squeeze if that activity lost its favoured status for policy loans. At the same time, as the government used export performance in the previous year as the criteria for renewal of a General Trading Company status, some Chaebol groups actively tried to take over some good small and medium-sized firms in diverse area of business.

It is interesting to compare Korean Chaebol with Japanese industrial groups. Despite their external similarities, Japanese industrial groups, called Keiretsu, are quite different from Korean Chaebol in some important respects.

First, the ownership structure of the groups is different. Although the earlier Japanese Zaibatsu were more like Chaebol in that they were controlled by the founder-families, the present Keiretsu were formed rather arbitrarily after the second World War. Their ownership is dispersed widely among the public and they are controlled and managed by professional managers, whilst in Korea, in addition to the family ownership, members of the family actively participate in the management of the companies (see Steers, Shin and Ungson 1989).

Second, Japanese Keiretsu are formed around in-house commercial banks, the so-called main banks, with equity participation between the main bank and the affiliated firms. The main bank monitors the affiliated firms on a long-term basis, and even when a firm is in financial distress, the main bank will often extend the maturity of loans as it is to their advantage to rescue the firm rather than make it bankrupt. In this way, the main bank mitigates some of the information problems that the firms might face in the credit market.

In the Korean Chaebol groups, there are no in-house commercial banks. Rather, in the 1960s and 1970s, the government arranged long-term relationships by intervening in the banking sector, and therefore the preferential treatment of certain firms or investment projects by a bank was not based on profit incentives between the bank and the firm but relied on the expectation that the government would recover any losses involved.

In the 1980s, each Chaebol group has been assigned a 'main bank', which does not however have any equity relationship with the companies. This Korean main bank system was an invention of the government in order to regulate the total amount of borrowing by the 50 largest Chaebol groups.[19] This arrangement was a part of government industrial policy. The 'main banks' are regulated by the Bank of Korea Supervisory Board, which is itself tightly controlled by the Ministry of Finance.

Although the dual structure of the Korean corporate sector has resulted from the government's selective credit policy in the 1960s and 1970s, and also in the early 1980s, this structure seems to have become more consolidated as we move into the 1980s. In the 1980s, we observe that group firms increasingly used measures such as cross payment guarantees among affiliated firms to facilitate borrowing from the banks, effectively creating an internal capital market among the member firms.[20] As the government took initiatives to liberalise the financial markets and open them to more competitive forces in the 1980s, the Chaebol groups could no longer rely on the ready availability of favourable long-term finance as has previously been the case, and therefore sought ways to exploit their advantages in the new environment. It is also the case that the Chaebol groups have increased their ownership of non-bank financial intermediaries and local banks in this period, for similar reasons.

In comparison to its treatment of Chaebol groups and large firms, the government has kept an arms-length relationship with small and medium-sized firms. This discriminatory treatment of the corporate sector by the government presented the latter with many problems. First, small and medium-sized firms were rationed out of bank credit or had to borrow from the banks at a far higher cost and provide collateral, or borrow from the curb market at even much higher rates. Second, because of poor access to capital, they had difficulty in exploiting profitable investment opportunities when they arouse. Since the Chaebol groups were the main beneficiaries of selection government intervention, it is expected that mainly non-Chaebol group companies would suffer from these same problems.

The heterogeneous financing environment facing these two distinct groups of companies in the 'dual' industrial structure was certainly more severe in the 1960s and 1970s, when the policy of financial repression was at its peak. It is recognised that in the 1980s the government made efforts to improve the availability of investment finance for the less favoured firms. Nevertheless it is expected that Chaebol firms would continue to enjoy important advantages in the 1980s, partly as the legacy of the government's previous intervening policies, and partly as a results of the slow pace at which the liberalisation policy actually proceeds.

2.5 Concluding remarks

In this chapter, we have described the Korean financial system and its relationship both with the Korean industrial structure and with the financial structure of Korean corporations. We argued that after more than two decades of targeted government intervention in the allocation of investment finance, there has developed a sustainable structure in which the financing of investment by certain corporations remains systematically different from the financing of other corporations which do not share their key characteristics. In particular, Chaebol firms and large firms have enjoyed cheaper access to loan finance than non-Chaebol affiliated firms and smaller firms. At least historically, this has reflected differences in the abilities of these firms to export and to operate in heavier industries.

Table 2.1 Growth of the financial sector in Korea

(percent)

	1965	1970	1975	1980	1985	1990
M1/GNP	-	-	11.7	10.4	10.4	9.5
M2/GNP	12.1	35.0	31.3	34.2	39.2	40.8
M3/GNP	-	-	36.0	48.6	75.2	114.8
Domestic credit/GNP	-	-	39.5	45.8	58.4	56.1
Corporate bond/GNP	-	-	-	4.5	10.0	7.0
Deposit share						
Banks	-	-	82.1	69.9	53.7	41.2
NBFIs	-	-	17.9	30.1	46.3	58.8
National saving/GNP	7.4	15.7	18.2	23.1	29.1	35.5
Stock market Capitalization/GNP	-	-	-	6.9	9.0	60.6

Source: Ministry of Finance, *Fiscal and Financial Statistics*, various issues.

Notes: M1 is defined as currency in circulation plus the demand deposits at monetary institutions; M2 as M1 plus the time and savings deposits and resident's foreign currency deposits at monetary institutions; and M3 as M2 plus deposits at NBFIs and commercial bills sold and certificates of deposits and debentures issued by deposit-taking banks.

Table 2.2 Trend of interest rates and inflation in Korea

(annual percentage)

	Bank time deposit	General bank loan	Corporate bond yield	Curb market rate	GNP deflator
1965	18.8	-	-	58.8	6.2
1966	30.0	-	-	58.7	14.5
1970	22.8	24.0	-	49.8	15.6
1975	15.0	15.5	20.1	41.3	25.2
1976	15.5	16.5	20.4	40.5	21.2
1977	15.8	17.3	20.1	38.1	16.6
1978	16.7	17.7	21.1	41.2	22.8
1979	18.6	19.0	26.7	42.4	19.6
1980	22.7	23.4	30.1	44.9	24.0
1981	19.3	19.8	24.4	35.3	16.9
1982	10.9	12.5	17.3	30.6	7.1
1983	8.0	10.0	14.2	25.8	5.0
1984	9.1	10.6	14.1	24.8	3.9
1985	10.0	11.5	14.2	24.0	4.2
1986	10.0	11.5	12.8	23.1	2.7
1987	10.0	11.5	12.8	23.0	3.4
1988	10.0	11.5	14.5	22.7	5.9
1989	10.0	11.5	15.2	19.1	5.2
1990	10.0	11.5	16.4	18.7	10.6

Source: quoted from Nam (1992)

Table 2.3 Growth of Korean stock market

	1980	1985	1990	1991
Number of listed companies	352	342	669	686
Total market value of capital (billion won)	2,526	6,570	79,019	73,117
(as % of GNP)	6.9	9.0	60.6	51.6
Total trading volume (billion won)	1134	3620	54354	62564
Stock index	106.9	163.4	696.1	611.0
P/E ratio	2.6	5.2	12.8	10.4

Source: quoted from Amsden and Euh (1993)

Table 2.4 The share of Chaebols in the Korean manufacturing sector

(percent)

Group	Sales			Employment			Value added	
	1978	1982	1985	1978	1982	1985	1982	1985
Top 5	15.7	22.6	23.0	9.5	8.4	9.7	17.4	18.7
Top 10	21.2	30.2	30.2	13.9	12.2	11.4	23.1	24.2
Top 20	29.3	36.6	36.4	18.2	16.0	15.5	29.4	34.4
Top 30	34.1	40.7	40.2	22.2	18.6	17.6	33.2	39.6

Source: quoted from Lee (1990)

Notes

1. These firms were the founders of some of the Chaebol industrial groups which would dominate the economic scene for the next three decades. Their business areas were in textiles, chemical products, food, machinery, and metal products. For more detail, see Choi (1993).
2. Although the informal sector is regarded as having shrinked over the periods, some financial scandals in the 1980s and the abolition of unassumed name accounts in 1993 suggest that the size of informal sector is sizeable. The dual structure of Korean financial sector was detailed in Cole and Park (1983).
3. The Monetary Board of the Bank of Korea is tightly controlled by the Ministry of Finance on its decisions over monetary policy and interest rates. For more detail, see Cole and Park (1983).
4. The main purpose of the decree was to freeze the level of corporate debt from the informal money market (curb market). The detail will be discussed in later sections.
5. World Bank (1989) observes that the curb market has been closely integrated with the formal market.

6. This policy was implemented to the recommendation of the US AID commission, advised by Gurly, Patrick and Shaw.
7. Nam (1992) suggests two reasons. First, the government was concerned that the emergence of other developing countries in Asia posed a serious threat to Korea's continued export-growth. Second, it felt a need to establish its own defence industry, faced with a possible pull-out of US armed forces.
8. In the 1960s and 1970s, capital inflows and outflows were tightly controlled to support this low interest rate policy.
9. Cole and Park (1983) specified two reasons of why this was significant. First, it marked the end of the partial financial liberalization policy started in 1965 and a return to the financial repression of previous years. Second, it relieved the financial burden of firms at the expense of banks and the public at large.
10. From 1986, rediscount facilities for foreign banking operations began to be available under the same conditions applied to domestic banks, and the number of the foreign bank branches has more than doubled in the course of the 1980s (see Lee 1988). However, foreign investors were not allowed to purchase individual stocks in the Korean stock market until early 1992 (see Nam 1992).
11. Before these measures, the government owned 20-30 percent of the total shares of these commercial banks and, at the same time, the voting power of any one private shareholder was limited to a maximum 10 percent regardless of their shareholding, so that the government exercised effective control (see Nam 1992).
12. In the 1960s and 1970s, the size of the stock market was relatively small because of lack of interest from both the demand and the supply side. First, large firms in Korea were reluctant to go public as it meant diluting the concentrated ownership by the founder-families and at the same time firms, especially large Chaebol group firms, found it more attractive to borrow from banks than to raise funds from new equity issues in the stock market, because borrowing from banks enabled them to share downside risk with the government. Second, it was a general perception that

buying stocks in the Korean stock market involved excessive risk, because stock prices were thought to be manipulated by a small number of 'big' hands and fair access to information was unlikely to be the case (Cho 1994).

13. Despite this, it should be stressed that the Korean bond market has remained relatively underdeveloped. Most corporate bonds are issued under the guarantee of financial institutions, especially the nationwide commercial banks; therefore they are, more or less, an extended form of commercial bank loans. Cho (1994) argues that the increasing issuance of bonds in Korea in the 1980s should be regarded as a second-best choice for firms due to the shortage of loanable funds from banks.
14. Short-term export loans by commercial banks were automatically approved to those who had received export letters of credit. In 1976 the law was amended to benefit only those whose exports exceeded $30 million, which favoured established exporters (see Choi 1993).
15. By 1966 total foreign loans guarantee were almost equal to the total of outstanding bank loans; the domestic and foreign credits were 14.4 and 14.0 % of the GNP respectively (see Cole and Park 1983).
16. In 1972, the political dictatorship strengthened as the president changed the Constitution so that he could be elected three times. To soften the public animosity toward the regime, the government proposed a bold new economic plan.
17. This point was also made by Chowdhury and Islam (1992).
18. Korean Chaebol groups such as Samsung, Daewoo and Hyundai are famous for making everything from ships and automobiles to micro chips and TVs.
19. The Korean-style main bank system has been used as a tool with which the government collects information on Chaebol firms and controls their business activities, so that any harmful effects of economic concentration are minimised (See Nam and Kim 1995). They

used the term 'principal transactions bank' instead of 'main bank' for Korea.

20. This point was mentioned in Cho (1989) and Lee (1992).

3 The pattern of investment finance in Korea: Evidence from aggregate data

3.1 Introduction

In this chapter, we investigate the pattern of investment finance in the Korean corporate sector using aggregate level flow of funds data. The main objectives of this analysis are to document how physical investment in the corporate sector is financed, how this has developed over the last fifteen years and how this compares to patterns of investment finance in the major G7 economies.

In the recent literature, there has been growing interest in comparing the patterns of investment finance in different countries (e.g. Mayer 1988 1990, Mayer and Alexander 1990, Corbett and Jenkinson 1994). These studies rely on flow analysis rather than on stock analysis. Calculating various ratios which indicate the relationship between stocks of debt and assets, such as the gearing ratio, forms the central part of international comparative studies of corporate financing which rely on stock analysis. As we discuss, the stock-based analysis does not adequately answer our main research question, 'How was new physical investment financed?', owing to problems such as the effects of inflation and uncertainty. We adopt the methodologies used in the above mentioned literature in calculating the shares of different sources of finance from flow data, first to have a clear picture of how physical investment was actually financed from various financial sources, then to study how the variation in the use of different financial sources was affected by the development of financial institutions and markets in Korea, and further to compare our results with those from other countries.

In the next section, we will discuss methodological issues, explaining the flow approach and the reasons we use it, and why we calculate the contribution of different sources of finance on both a gross and a net basis. This is followed by a section which outlines the nature of the data used in this chapter. Details of the construction of the measures are presented in Appendix 3.3. In section 3.4, we analyse the financing of investment in both the Korean corporate sector and the manufacturing sector over the last fifteen years, and also examine the trends in corporate financing over successive five year periods. In section 3.5, we will compare the results of our study of Korean corporate finance patterns with the results from other studies, particularly Mayer (1988,1990) and Corbett and Jenkinson (1994). Finally, we summarise the main findings and draw some implications of this analysis.

3.2 Methodological issues

To obtain a picture of the financial structure of an economy or company, it is traditional to use various financial ratios such as gearing ratios and profit ratios. However, Mayer (1988,1990) argued that this stock-based approach has inherent drawbacks and is not appropriate for studies whose focus is on the sources of finance for physical investment. He emphasized that this is particularly the case for international comparison of financial systems. In this section, we will briefly review the advantages of the flow-based approach compared to the stock-based approach. This discussion is based on Mayer (1988,1990) and Corbett and Jenkinson (1994).

Stock vs flow approaches

Gearing ratios have often been used to study financing patterns in different countries. As the gearing ratio is measured from balance sheet data at a point in time, this evidence cannot properly address questions about the patterns of investment finance over a particular period of time. Since physical investment is itself conceptually a flow, we require a corresponding flow concept of finance.

In addition to this conceptual problem, Mayer (1988,1990) raised some doubts about using stock-related financial ratios as the basis for international comparison of financial systems. First, the practice of historic cost accounting in many countries causes the capital stock and equity valuation to be underestimated to an extent which depends on the history of inflation. This problem becomes more severe because the frequency of asset revaluations is different in different countries.[1] To correct this problem, some authors suggest using market valuations of assets and debt to calculate the gearing ratio (Aoki, 1984 and Borio 1990). However, market valuations of debt, equity and capital reflect not only inflows and outflows of debt and equity finance, but also changes in the valuation of existing capital assets as a result of the arrival of new information (Corbett and Jenkinson 1994). Second, book values of assets and reserves are sensitive to depreciation rules, and accounting conventions on depreciation vary across countries.[2] This difference partly reflects differences in corporate tax regimes across countries, and also whether differences are permitted between commercial depreciation provisions and fiscal depreciation schedules.

For these reasons, in our study, we prefer to adopt flow-based methods rather than stock-based methods.[3] By adopting the flow approach, we will benefit from comparing our results to the findings of other studies which have used similar techniques to make an international comparison of financing patterns.

The flow approach: gross and net sources

To calculate flow measures of the sources of investment finance we make use of flow of funds accounts, either for a whole sector or for an individual company, which show the sources and uses of funds over a particular time period. On the sources side, internal sources and external sources of finance are recorded; and on the uses side, the amounts of physical investment and financial investment are recorded. Total sources and total uses are bound to be equal by accounting identity.

We report the proportions of different sources of finance on both a gross and a net basis. For the corporate sector as a whole, the gross financing figures are calculated as a share of the total sources that the corporate sector raised internally and externally. The net financing figures are calculated as a proportion of total physical investment (including inventories), after netting out the accumulation of financial assets from the corresponding increase in liabilities. Although the detail of our calculations will be presented in Appendix 3.3, we present in Table 3.1 the structure of gross and net of finance schematically.

In Table 3.1, the gross sources of finance are items (1)-(6). These will each be reported as a proportion of total sources of finance, item (7). To obtain the net sources of finance, items (10)-(13) on the uses side are subtracted from the corresponding items on the sources side. These will each be reported as a proportion of total physical investment (item (8)+(9)).

What are the main advantages of calculating these net sources of finance?

First, by calculating the net figures we can identify the contribution of each financing source to the overall financing of physical investment.

Second, we are able to identify the net contribution of new equity.[4] In the UK and US, firms commonly use their resources to buy equity in other firms, either to protect themselves from possible takeover or to take over other firms. Thus, it is quite usual that the net figure for equity finance is much smaller than the corresponding gross figure in these countries. In contrast, in Japan, this takeover activity is comparatively rare. Also in Korea, the hostile takeover of one firm by another firm is scarcely heard of, although takeovers prompted by government or bank intervention often take place. By comparing the gross and net figures for new equity finance, we may investigate whether there has been substantial accumulation of equity on the uses side related to this takeover activity.

Third, distortions resulting from the practice of compensating balances can be avoided by calculating the net contribution of loans. In the US and Japan, it is common that banks require the borrower to deposit some fraction of the value of a loan at the same bank. As a result, the borrower can actually borrow less than the gross value of the loan. In Korea, this practice has existed in an even more severe form, partly as a consequence of government regulation of lending rates and deposit rates.

Weighted averages or unweighted averages?

Mayer (1988,1990) suggested that the share of each financing source should be calculated on a weighted average basis. These shares of different sources of finance can be calculated by first revaluing all sources of finance into constant prices, and then taking the weighted average of shares over different years.[5] Where possible, we adopt this method of calculation in the analysis below.

The alternative is to calculate the shares of each source of finance in each year, and then take the unweighted average of these shares across years. The main advantage of weighted averages over unweighted averages is that this gives each year an appropriate weight, by taking into account the amount of total finance or total investment in the case of gross or net sources, respectively. In this way the pattern of finance in years of high investment is given a higher weight. On the whole we will adopt the weighted average method to calculate the share of each source of finance, but we are required by a data limitation to use the unweighted average method for one of the data sets studied in this chapter. This issue will be further discussed in the next section.

3.3 Description of the data

There are two main data sources used in this chapter: aggregate flow of funds data for the whole corporate sector, obtained from National Accounts; and manufacturing sector flow of funds data, obtained by aggregating a representative sample of company accounts data. Both data sets are published by the Bank of Korea under the title of the National Accounts and the Financial Statement Analysis respectively. Before we describe these data sets in more detail, we will briefly review the characteristics of alternative sources of flow of funds data. This discussion is based on Mayer (1990).

Evaluation of alternative data sources

There are basically two sources of flow of funds data that can be used in the study of financing patterns: aggregate or sectoral flow of funds accounts, and company accounts data. The former are usually obtained from National Income Accounts; the latter relate to individual firms, but are sometimes published in an aggregated form.[6] As these two kinds of data are both used in this chapter, several points on the pros and cons of these different sources should be noted.

First, while the coverage of companies in aggregate flow of funds data is comprehensive, the company accounts samples available can sometimes be quite limited in their coverage. Company accounts data are also difficult to compare across countries due to international differences in accounting conventions. However, the problem of international comparability is not entirely avoided by using the aggregate flow of funds data; despite the general adoption of Standard National Accounting (SNA) conventions, there remain some international differences in the precise definitions of sectors and transactions.

Second, company accounts record the whole operations of a company, which may cover the activity of foreign subsidiaries on a world-wide consolidated basis.[7] In contrast, national flow of funds accounts only cover domestic operations. For these reasons, it may be said that the former source is more appropriate for analysing how the corporate sector funds itself, while the latter source is more relevant for examining the contribution of the domestic financial systems.

In this chapter, we use both aggregate flow of funds accounts for the corporate sector from National Accounts, and aggregated company accounts of firms in the manufacturing sector.

Aggregate flow of funds data

Aggregate flow of funds data is obtained from the National Accounts of Korea, published by the Bank of Korea. The data period covers from 1975 to 1990. The particular part of the flow of funds table used here is the Capital Finance Account of the non-financial business sector, the basic structure of which is given in Appendix 3.1.

This account combines both non-financial accounts and financial accounts. The former shows the amount of physical investment and the amount of internal funds used to finance this investment. The difference between these two figures is called 'net borrowing'. Theoretically, this difference should be the same as the gap between the change in assets and the change in liabilities in the financial transaction accounts, which is called 'net lending'. But because the two accounts were calculated from different data sources, there may in fact be some discrepancy between the 'net borrowing' and 'net lending' figures. The Capital Finance Account provides valuable information on how much physical investment has been undertaken in aggregate, and a detailed picture of how it was financed from various internal and external sources.

The non-financial business sector here includes both publicly-owned firms and private firms. The former includes wholly-owned government firms and partially-owned government firms. The latter is composed of corporate firms and non-corporate firms whose main activities are non-financial.

There are two minor points to be noted about this data. First, although the financial transaction account provides separate figures for government and private firms, the non-financial transaction account does not differentiate between these two groups. For this reason, a separate analysis could not be undertaken for government and private firms. Secondly, we chose to use the period 1975-1990 because before 1975 government firms are not included in the corporate sector, and the format of the data is also different between pre-1975 and post-1975 periods.

Manufacturing flow of funds data

The Bank of Korea also reports information from the company accounts of the Korean corporate sector, in an aggregated form, under the title 'Financial Statement Analysis'. From the population of firms which report information for corporate tax purposes[8] to the Korea Tax Bureau (44,134 firms as of 1986) is selected the sample of firms for analysis, which amounted to 2,868 firms as of 1989. From 1979, this sample has been modified every three years to make sure that the sample represents the population accurately. The Bank collects information from the published company accounts of these sample firms and aggregates it to produce aggregated company accounts for various samples of Korean companies.

Financial Statement Analysis reports company accounts for industries classified according to the Korea Standard Industry Code (KSIC). Company accounts are also available for sub-samples of large and small firms in each industry group, classified according to whether the firm has more than 300 full-time employees or not. For our analysis, we focus on the flow of funds data for the whole manufacturing sector, which is also divided into large and small firms. From 1973, Financial Statement Analysis provides separate information for further interesting sub-samples, such as exporting and domestic companies, and companies in heavy and light industries within the manufacturing sector.

Two qualifications should be noted as to the calculation of gross and net sources of finance using this manufacturing flow of funds data.

First, for this data set, we calculated the gross and net shares of finance on an unweighted average basis. This is due to the fact that the number of firms in the sample has increased considerably over the period[9] and therefore weighted average figures based on total investment for the sample in each year would not be appropriate. We calculate unweighted averages of the shares of each sources of finance across the sample period (1975-1990). It should be noted that the gross shares of each source of finance, that are published for each year in Financial Statement Analysis, are themselves calculated on a weighted average basis across the sample of firms.

Second, again in contrast to the aggregate flow of funds data, no separate figures are reported for financial investment in new equities and bonds. Therefore, we cannot report separate net shares for new equity and bonds, and instead we report a single figure for the net contribution of securities. On top of this problem, financial investment in securities is aggregated with other financial investment such as long-term loans and notes receivable and leasehold rights on the uses side of the flow of funds accounts. This data limitation makes it likely that the net share of finance from securities will be underestimated because inappropriate items have also been netted off against the gross amount of securities issued. The extent of this problem will be considered in section 4.4 of the next chapter, where individual company accounts which provide separate figures for other financial investment used.

3.4 The pattern of corporate financing in Korea: 1975-1990

In this section, both aggregate and manufacturing flow of funds data are used to describe how investment has been financed in Korea. The method used to calculate these figures is described in Appendix 3.3, and follows as closely as possible the methods used by Mayer (1988,1990) and Corbett and Jenkinson (1994).

Evidence from aggregate flow of funds data

Tables 3.2 and 3.3 present, respectively, the gross and net sources of finance calculated from aggregate National Accounts data for the non-financial business sector. The period covered by our data is 1975 to 1990, and is divided into three sub-periods. A number of observations emerge from these tables.

First, the importance of internally generated funds was increasing over this period.[10] On the gross basis, we observe that the importance of retentions exceeded that of loans in the second half of the 1980s; and on the net basis, retentions were clearly the single largest source of finance. This may indicate that the Korean corporate sector has become more profitable and less reliant on external financing , particularly on bank loans, to finance its investment. However, the net figure of 46.4 % for retentions for this period as a whole is still relatively low compared to other countries, such as the US and the UK and even Japan. A detailed international comparison will be presented in section 3.5.

Second, the share of new equity and bonds increased on both the gross and the net basis. One interesting point here is that the shares of bonds and particularly new equity are higher on the net basis. Mayer (1988) showed that in the US and UK, the share of finance from securities is significantly lower on the net basis, compared to the gross basis. This may be due to the fact that Korean companies have relatively few securities on the asset side of their balance sheets, because they are much less involved in takeover and merger activities than companies in the US and the UK.

From the middle of the 1980s, the equity and bond markets emerged as important financial markets in Korea. The number of companies listed on the stock market increased from 189 at the end of 1975 to 626 at the end of 1989. Behind the scene, the government was very keen to encourage firms to go public and to promote the stock market for two reasons. First, the United States was putting pressure on the Korean government to open its financial markets to international investors within a short period of time, and therefore the government was anxious to enlarge and strengthen the domestic stock market. Second, the government made an effort to decrease the financial leverage of firms, especially 'Chaebol' firms. Despite this background, the figures in Tables 3.2 and 3.3 do not suggest a very dramatic increase in the importance of new equity finance. However, this may be reconciled by the fact that the National Accounts data covers not only quoted firms but also unquoted firms, and the new equity figure here also includes the capital participation in government-owned firms.

Third, the proportion of loans as a source of finance has declined in the 1980s, although not consistently over our whole sample period. Compared to the latter half of the 1970s, the share of loans increased in the early 1980s. This becomes more clear in Figure 3.1, which shows the time-series of the shares of retention and loan financing on a net basis. The proportion of loan financing rose sharply in the period 1978-79 and then declined over the 1980s. This abrupt increase in loan financing may have been caused by the macroeconomic environment which firms were exposed to after the second oil shock in the late 1970s. What is also interesting in Figure 3.1 is that the shares of retention and loan financing are negatively correlated in a consistent way.[11]

Sussman (1994) has discussed this inverse association between the shares of internal finance and loan finance, and suggested that fluctuations in both may be driven by the overall demand for investment. That is, when investment demand is high, a lower proportion can be financed from internal sources, and the share of loan finance increases to fill the gap. The time series for investment by the non-financial business sector (in constant prices) is presented in Figure 3.1. We note that whilst the big rise in investment in 1990 is indeed associated with an increase in the share financed by loans, the peak in the loan finance series in 1980 was not associated with a strong increase in investment.

Fourth, the share of foreign debt has decreased to a great extent. Bank of Korea (1990) documents that foreign borrowing constituted a vital source of finance in the earlier stages of economic development, accounting for as much as 38 % of total external funds raised by the corporate sector in the latter half of the 1960s. The proportion of foreign debt decreased from 10.0 % on the net basis in the late 1970s to 0.1 % in the late 1980s. This fall reflected the rapid growth of domestic financial markets and the government's efforts to reduce short-term foreign debts, as well as the steady increase in domestic foreign exchange holdings with economic growth.

The above discussion is based on weighted averages for the shares of different sources of finance. We also present the unweighted averages in Appendix 3.2 so that comparison with the results from the manufacturing flow of funds data can be made on a similar basis. The comparison of these two sets of results shows that unweighted averages are in fact very close to the weighted average figures. However, it can be noted that the weighted average figures tend to produce slightly higher shares for retentions, new equity and bonds, and a sightly lower share for loan finance. This occurs because the weighted averages give more weight to the later years of the sample.

Evidence from manufacturing sector flow of funds data

Tables 3.4 and 3.5 present gross and net sources of finance calculated from the manufacturing sector flow of funds data. This data set covers a narrower range of firms than the aggregate flow of funds data, in that it does not include government-owned firms and non-manufacturing firms. By comparison with the corporate sector as a whole,[12] manufacturing firms used a lower share of finance from new equity and bonds, and higher shares of finance from internal funds and loans over the period 1975-90. These differences are especially noticeable when considering the net sources of finance. We can, however, observe some similar trends in the shares of different sources of finance over time.

First, the share of retentions has increased on average over the period for both data sets. Over the three five-year sub-periods it is observed that both the gross and net share of retentions have increased more sharply for the manufacturing sector than for the whole corporate sector.

Second, the gross share of finance from new share issues maintains a stable level over the whole period. In contrast, the gross share of finance from bonds doubled between the late 1970s and the late 1980s. This pattern is in line with the evidence for the share of bonds in gross finance in the aggregate data. However the net share of finance from these securities[13] has decreased in the manufacturing sector, which is in contrast to the increase in the net share of finance from new equity and bonds for the business sector as a whole. The increased use of finance from the securities markets seems to have been concentrated outside the manufacturing sector.

It should be noted that, as we discussed in section 3.3, the net share of securities finance is likely to be underestimated here as other financial investment has also been netted off against the gross funds raised from new equities and bonds to calculate the net figure. In Chapter 4, we will be able to distinguish other financial investment from financial investment in new equities and bonds, and consequently the resulting net share of finance from securities will be measured more accurately.

Third, the share of loans has declined over this period on both the gross and the net basis. The change in the composition of loans in the period 1980-84 is also noteworthy. The sharp fall in the share of long-term loans (maturity greater than one year) to 7.8 % on a gross basis in the early 1980s may reflect the Korean government's effort to reduce the flow of privileged loans to certain sectors and firms, as non-performing loans accumulated in the banking sector (see Cho 1989). The temporary increase in the share of short-term loans (maturity less than one year) may be associated with the increase in loans from non-bank sources shown in Table 3.2.

Fourth, trade credit made a negative contribution to the net sources of finance for investment, particularly in the first half of the 1980s. This indicates that manufacturing firms were net lenders to other firms on a trade credit basis.

The main advantage of using this flow of funds data for firms in the manufacturing sector is that we can consider differences in the pattern of corporate finance according to size and other characteristics of firms. First, the firms are divided into two size categories, according to whether their average number of full-time employees each year is over 300 or not Second, the firms are divided into export firms and domestic firms, according to whether the ratio of exports to total output is over 50 % or not. The firms are also divided into heavy industry and light industry sectors. We will examine the financing patterns for each of these sub-samples in turn.

In Table 3.6 we present the sources of finance for large firms and small firms in the manufacturing sector. According to these figures, the large firms had a somewhat higher share of retentions, and were less reliant on loans than small firms to finance their investment. It is often the case that small firms, most of which are relatively young firms, tend to expand quickly without much accumulated profit, hence causing them to rely more on external financing, especially bank borrowing. In this data, as firms were classified as 'small' if the number of employees is under 300, this scenario may well apply.

Another point may be noted on the figures for bond financing. The data on gross sources shows that the share of bonds is much higher for larger firms than for smaller firms. Superior access to bond markets for larger firms may reflect the fact that more information is available about the performance and prospects of large firms, with default risk also being lower.

The comparison of the maturity structure of loans is also of some interest. The data on gross sources suggests a higher share of short-term loans, especially for smaller firms. However, the data on net sources indicates equal proportions of short-term loans and long-term loans, for both size classes. This illustrates the importance of compensating balances in the Korean banking system, and suggests that these have been particularly high for smaller companies.

In Table 3.7 we present the sources of finance for export firms and domestic firms. The share of retentions is very similar for both sub-samples, with no large differences between the shares of other financing sources, except that export firms have a higher share of loans. Perhaps surprisingly, the export firms were particularly reliant on short-term loans.

In Table 3.8 we present the sources of finance for firms in heavy and light industries. The data on net sources indicates that firms in heavy industries used a higher proportion of finance from securities, and the data on gross sources suggest that this was particularly the case for finance from new equity. Otherwise the pattern of investment finance was very similar between these sectors.

3.5 Comparisons with other studies

In this section, we will compare our results for Korea with those for other countries where similar studies have been reported. At the outset, we made sure that we used similar methods for calculating the shares of different sources of finance, so as to be able to make an international comparison between our results and those from previous studies. We will compare both gross and net sources of finance in Korea with four other major countries: the United Kingdom, United States, Germany and Japan. The financial systems in these countries are often said to represent one of two typical financial systems. The financial system in the US and UK is usually characterised as 'market-based' and that in Germany and Japan is characterised as 'bank-based'. The market-based systems are typically regarded as having developed equity and bond markets, which play an important role in improving the allocative efficiency of the economy, through activities such as takeovers and mergers. In contrast, in the bank-based systems firms finance a higher share of investment through bank loans and often, in such cases, there are equity participations relating firms and banks. However, recent studies of the sources of finance for investment have suggested that this traditional classification of financial systems may need to be modified.

Gross sources of finance

Table 3.9 shows the average gross sources of finance for the non-financial business sector in Korea and in four other countries, over the periods 1975-1990 and 1970-1990 respectively. These figures are all derived from flow of funds data for the corporate sector in the National Income Accounts. The figures for Korea are taken from Table 3.2, whilst those for other countries are from Corbett and Jenkinson (1994).

Corbett and Jenkinson (1994) document the main features of corporate finance in the first four countries as follows.

First, the gross figures show that in all four countries, internal funds are the single most important source of finance. The share of retentions in Japan is lowest at 40 % of total gross sources, but there is a similar level of around 60 % in the other three countries. Second, the equity and bond markets provide relatively insignificant shares of gross finance in all countries, although the proportion of bond financing in the US is far higher than in the other countries.[14] These two points were previously observed by Mayer (1988,1990). Mayer (1990) points out that in none of the countries examined did the securities markets play a significant part in financing investment in the corporate sector, and in most cases loan financing accounted for a major share of external financing.

Third, the figures for the share of loan financing suggest that the biggest difference is between Japan and the three other countries. Japan is traditionally regarded as having a 'bank-based' financial system, and does indeed have the highest figure for loan financing; but the figure for Germany, which is lower than in the UK, comes as a surprise in the context of the conventional classification of financial systems.

It is also notable that there are marked differences between the US and the UK in the shares of bonds and loan financing, considering the suggestion that these two countries are supposed to have similar financial systems.

Based on these observations, Corbett and Jenkinson (1994) postulate that the classic distinction between bank-based and market-based systems, represented by Japan and Germany on the one hand and by the US and the UK on the other, needs to be modified. They also suggest that there has been some convergence over the last twenty years in the patterns of corporate finance in these countries. Sussman (1994) suggests that differences in the patterns of finance across countries may be partly explained by differences in the level of investment. Japan and the US, for example, had similar levels of profits as a share of output, but investment as a share of output was much higher in Japan. Therefore a smaller share of investment could be financed from internal sources, and a higher share had to be financed by borrowing.

We now compare the figures for these four countries with our results for Korea. The Korean figures are based on the flow of funds data from Korean National Accounts, which adopted the SNA (Standard National Accounts) standard. Although precise National Accounts practices do vary slightly between the countries, these figures should be broadly comparable.

Based on these figures for the gross sources of finance, the financing pattern in Korea appears to be most similar to that in Japan. The 30.0 % share of retentions is even lower than found in Japan, and the gross share of retentions was barely higher than the gross share of loans in Korea over this period. The share of loans is similar to that found in Japan, and much higher than found in other three countries. Nevertheless the share of finance from new equity and bonds was much higher in Korea than in Japan.

At the same time, we can observe important differences between the financing pattern in Korea and in the three other countries. First, for the share of retentions, Korea has much the lowest share in any of these five countries. However, as we observed in section 3.4, the share of internal funds in Korea did show a tendency to increase over the period. Second, the shares of both new equity and bonds are high by international standards.[15] The share of new equity is the highest of these five countries, and the share of bonds is second only to the US figure. This may reflect the emergence of these two financial markets in Korea over this period. Yet, the high share of loans, which is second only to Japan, suggests that banks have continued to play an important role in providing finance to the corporate sector in Korea.

In summary, on a gross basis, the financing pattern in Korea over this period was quite unique, having a resemblance only to the pattern found in Japan. Korea and Japan are similar in that the share of internal funds was low by international standards, and the share of loans was high, but Korea did not share the modest proportions of finance from new equity and bonds found in Japan.

Net sources of finance

Table 3.10 presents the net sources of finance for the non-financial business sector in Korea and in the other four countries. Corbett and Jenkinson (1994) note that while certain patterns found in the gross sources of finance continue to hold, there are some important differences.

First, the share of internal funds increases substantially in all four countries. In the US and UK, the net contribution of internal sources accounts for over 90 % of the financing of investment. The net contribution of internal funds remains lowest in Japan at 69 %.

Second, the net share of loans in Germany is the lowest of these four countries, and remains somewhat at odds with the traditional view of the German financial system, according to which bank plays a relatively important role in financing investment and thus the German financial system is classed as a 'bank-based' system. The net figure of 11 % for loans is even lower than found in the UK and US. Based on these findings, Corbett and Jenkinson (1994) question the typical division of financial systems in terms of bank or market dominance. Third, the contribution of new equity finance diminishes sharply in both the US and UK on a net basis, recording a negative contribution in both cases, while for Japan the net contribution of new equity finance is the highest among these four countries.[16]

The comparison with net sources of finance in Korea reinforces our previous observations based on gross sources of finance. Again we find that the share of retentions is the lowest in Korea, while the share of loans is comparable with Japan. On the other hand, the net contribution of finance from new equity and bonds was very high by international standards in Korea over this period, and considerably higher than that found in Japan.

3.6 Summary and conclusions

In this chapter we have analysed the patterns of investment finance in Korea and compared our findings with studies of the UK, US, Germany and Japan. For the corporate sector as a whole, we find that internal sources of funds have made a smaller contribution to the financing of investment in Korea than in any of these countries. This finding is consistent with the suggestion by Sussman (1994) that the share of internal sources and the level of investment are closely related, since the rate of investment in Korea over this period was higher even than in Japan. We also find that the contribution of internal funds was increasing in Korea over the period 1975-1990. As in Japan, we find that loan finance has played a major role in financing investment in Korea; but in contrast to Japan and all the other countries studied, we find that finance from new equity and bonds made a significant positive contribution in Korea.

We also analysed the pattern of investment finance in the Korean manufacturing sector. Manufacturing firms used a higher share of finance from internal sources and from loans, and a lower share of finance from new equity and bonds. Within manufacturing, larger firms (with more than 300 full-time employees) were found to use a higher share of internal funds and bonds, and a lower share of loans, than smaller firms. We did not find large differences in the pattern of investment finance between export and domestic firms, or between firms in heavy and light industries.

In the next chapter we will study the pattern of investment finance using individual company accounts data for a sample of large corporations that were quoted on the Korean stock market by the end of the 1980s. As well as providing a comparison with the aggregate results presented in this chapter, this will allow us to consider differences in the pattern of corporate finance between firms which belong to Chaebol groups and those which do not.

Table 3.1 Flow of funds[17]

	Gross Sources		**Gross Uses**
1.	internal funds	8.	physical investment
2.	new equity	9.	inventory investment
3.	bonds	10.	investment in equities
4.	short-term loans	11.	investment in bonds
5.	long-term loans	12.	trade advances
6.	trade credit	13.	cash and other deposits
7.	TOTAL SOURCES (1+2+3+4+5+6)	12.	TOTAL USES (8+9+10+11+12+13)

Net Sources	**Net Uses**
net internal funds (1)	total physical investment (8+9)
net new equity (2-10)	
net bonds (3-11)	
net short-term loans (4-13)	
net long-term loans (5)	
net trade credit (6-12)	
NET SOURCES (7-10-11-12-13)	

Table 3.2 Gross sources of finance for Korean non-financial firms
- Analysis of aggregate flow of funds data -

	75-79	80-84	85-90	75-90
retentions	22.8	26.3	33.6	30.0
new equity	10.7	11.5	13.9	12.8
bonds	5.1	11.0	14.3	12.0
loans	27.7	28.7	24.3	26.0
bank	17.1	13.0	12.5	13.4
non-bank	9.6	14.2	11.7	12.0
government	1.0	1.5	0.0	0.6
trade credit	11.3	10.8	5.5	7.8
foreign debt	8.8	3.6	2.1	3.5
other	13.5	8.0	6.3	7.9
total external	77.2	73.7	66.3	70.0

Table 3.3 Net sources of finance for Korean non-financial companies
- Analysis of aggregate flow of funds data -

	75-79	80-84	85-90	75-90
retentions	35.9	41.2	51.4	46.4
new equity	15.2	12.1	18.6	16.4
bonds	6.5	12.5	15.9	13.6
loans	29.0	33.7	18.1	23.8
trade credit	-0.0	-5.9	-4.6	-4.3
foreign debt	10.0	4.1	0.1	2.6
other	3.4	2.3	0.5	1.5
total external	64.1	58.8	48.6	53.6

Source of Tables 3.2 and 3.3: Bank of Korea, *National Accounts*, various issues.

Table 3.4 Gross sources of finance for Korean manufacturing firms
- Analysis of manufacturing flow of funds data -

	75-79	80-84	85-90	75-90
retentions	22.8	30.0	41.9	32.2
new equity	7.9	7.7	7.5	7.7
bonds	3.6	6.3	7.3	5.8
loans	37.7	27.8	23.2	29.1
short-term	18.4	20.0	12.7	16.7
long-term	19.3	7.8	10.5	12.4
trade credit	11.4	12.2	8.7	10.7
other	16.6	16.0	11.4	14.5
total external	77.2	70.0	58.1	67.8

Table 3.5 Net sources of finance for Korean manufacturing firms
- Analysis of manufacturing flow of funds data -

	75-79	80-84	85-90	75-90
retentions	34.9	54.3	66.5	52.8
securities (equity+bonds)	9.7	8.2	7.3	8.3
loans	48.3	41.3	30.5	39.5
short-term	18.5	26.6	13.8	19.3
long-term	29.8	14.7	16.7	20.2
trade credit	-1.6	-13.7	-6.6	-7.3
other	8.7	9.9	2.3	6.7
total external	65.1	45.7	33.5	47.2

Note to Tables 3.4 and 3.5: short-term loans if the maturity is less than 1 year and long-term loans otherwise.

Table 3.6 Sources of finance for large and small firms, 1975-90

	Gross sources			Net sources		
	All	Large	Small	All	Large	Small
retentions	32.2	33.1	27.8	52.8	53.9	47.9
new equity	7.7	7.6	8.6	8.3	8.6	8.2
bonds	5.8	6.5	2.3			
loans	29.1	28.7	32.6	39.5	38.6	41.5
short-term	16.7	16.2	21.1	19.3	19.2	21.0
long-term	12.4	12.5	11.5	20.2	19.4	20.5
total credit	10.7	9.2	16.2	-7.3	-8.4	-1.2
other	14.5	14.9	12.5	6.7	7.3	3.6
total external	67.8	66.9	72.2	47.2	46.1	52.1

Notes:

1) short-term loans if the maturity does not exceed 1 year and long-term loans otherwise.
2) large firms if the number of full-time employees is more than 300 and small firms otherwise.

Table 3.7 Sources of finance for export and domestic firms, 1975-90

	Gross sources		Net sources	
	Export	Domestic	Export	Domestic
retentions	32.9	31.4	51.5	53.2
new equity	7.2	7.7	7.3	8.4
bonds	5.2	6.4		
loans	31.0	28.4	43.0	38.0
short-term	19.8	15.1	25.0	16.7
long-term	11.2	13.2	18.1	21.3
trade credit	8.2	12.0	-5.2	-8.7
other	15.5	14.1	3.4	9.1
total external	67.1	68.6	48.5	46.8

Notes:

1) short-term loans if the maturity does not exceed 1 year and long-term loans otherwise.
2) export firms if the ratio of exports to total output is over 50 % and domestic firms otherwise.

Table 3.8 Sources of finance for firms in heavy and light industries 1975-90

	Gross sources		Net sources	
	Heavy	Light	Heavy	Light
retentions	32.0	32.7	52.5	53.7
new equity	9.3	5.5	10.3	4.5
bonds	5.7	5.8		
loans	28.9	29.2	39.6	39.0
short-term	15.1	18.6	17.7	21.2
long-term	13.8	10.5	21.9	17.8
trade credit	10.7	10.7	-7.3	-6.9
other	13.4	16.1	4.9	9.7
total external	68.0	67.3	47.5	46.3

Notes:

1) short-term loans if the maturity does not exceed 1 year and long-term loans otherwise.
2) refer to Appendix 3.1 for the industry classification.

Table 3.9 Gross sources of finance for five countries

	1970 - 89				1975 - 90
	UK	US	Germany	Japan	Korea
retentions	60.4	62.7	62.4	40.0	30.0
new equity	7.0	-4.9	2.3	3.9	12.8
bonds	2.3	12.8	0.9	3.9	12.0
loans	23.3	14.7	18.0	34.5	29.5
trade credit	1.9	8.8	1.8	15.6	7.8
other	5.2	5.9	14.6	2.1	7.9
total external	39.6	37.3	37.6	60.0	70.0

Table 3.10 Net sources of finance for five countries

	1970 - 89				1975 - 90
	UK	US	Germany	Japan	Korea
retentions	97.3	91.3	80.6	69.3	46.4
new equity	-10.4	-8.8	0.9	3.7	16.4
bonds	3.5	17.1	-0.6	4.7	13.6
loans	19.5	16.6	11.0	30.5	26.4
trade credit	-1.4	-3.7	-1.9	-8.1	-4.3
other	-8.4	-2.5	10.0	-0.1	1.5
total external	2.7	8.7	19.4	30.7	53.6

Source and notes to Tables 3.9 and 3.10:

Source: Corbett and Jenkinson (1994) and own calculations.

Notes: Capital transfers are incorporated into retentions and statistical adjustments into other sources. In calculating the retentions figure for Korea, capital transfers are also included. Loans here include foreign borrowing.

Appendix 3.1

Structure of Capital Finance Accounts

Non-financial transactions account

Savings Consumption of fixed capital Net capital tranfer 'Net borrowing'	Total fixed capital formation Increase in inventories Net acquisition of land and intangible assets
Finance	Accumulation

Fincial transaction account

Increase in financial liabilities	Increase in financial assets 'Net lending'
Sources	Uses

Criteria to classify firms

1) Large firms: the number of full time employees is over 300
   Small firms: the number of full time employees is below 300
2) Export firms: the proportion of exports in total sales is over 50 %
   Domestic firms: the proportion of exports in total sales below 50 %
3) Heavy and Chemical industries: industrial chemical, petroleum refineries, other non-metallic products (structural clay products, cement, lime, plaster, and concrete products) basic metal, fabricated metal products, machinery and equipment, electrical, electronic machinery and appliances, medical, photographic and optical measuring and controlling equipment and goods.
   Light industries: industries not classified as heavy and chemical industries.

Appendix 3.2: Unweighted average results

Table A.3.1 Gross sources of finance for Korean non-financial firms - Analysis of aggregate flow of funds data-

	75-79	80-84	85-90	75-90
retentions	22.7	26.0	35.3	28.5
new equity	11.3	11.5	13.5	12.2
bonds	4.7	11.0	12.6	9.6
loans	25.9	28.6	24.1	26.1
bank	15.8	13.1	13.6	14.3
non-bank	9.1	14.0	9.6	10.9
government	1.0	1.5	0.1	0.9
trade credit	10.8	11.0	5.9	9.0
foreign debt	10.0	3.9	1.8	5.0
other	14.4	8.0	6.9	9.6
total external	77.3	74.0	64.7	71.5

Table A.3.2 Net sources of finance for Korean non-financial firms
- Analysis of aggregate flow of funds data -

	75-79	80-84	85-90	75-90
retentions	35.8	40.5	53.8	43.0
new equity	16.3	12.1	17.9	15.6
bonds	5.9	12.6	14.4	11.2
loans	26.1	33.9	18.8	26.8
trade credit	-0.0	-5.7	-5.1	-3.8
foreign debt	11.9	4.7	-1.1	4.8
other	4.3	1.8	1.3	2.4
total external	64.2	59.5	46.2	57.0

Source of Tables A.3.1 and A.3.2: Bank of Korea, *National Accounts*, various issues.

Appendix 3.3

Table A.3.3 Aggregate flow of funds data: gross sources

Sources	Contents and Notes
Retentions	savings plus consumption of fixed capital plus net capital tranfer
New equity	new share issues plus capital participation in government firms
Bonds	short-term bonds and long-term bonds. New bond issues include convertible bonds and stock warrants
Loans	Bank of Korea loans, bank loans plus non-bank loans
Trade credit	short-term and long-term payables plus deferred liabilities
Foreign debt	foreign debt exclusive of foreign exchange holdings
Other	other accounts payable and accrued payables and other current liabilities. This item includes statistical adjustment

Table A.3.4 Aggregate flow of funds data: net sources

Sources	Contents and Notes
Retentions	same as gross figure
New equity	gross minus investment in new shares
Bonds	gross minus investment in bonds
Loans	gross minus cash and other deposits (the holding of domestic currency, demand and time deposits, non-residential deposits)

Trade credit	gross less short-term and long-term receivables and deferred assets
Foreign debt	gross minus the foreign asset and currency
Other	gross minus other accounts receivable and accrued receivables and other current assets

Table A.3.5 Manufacturing flow of funds data: gross sources

Sources	**Contents and Notes**
Retentions	retained earnings plus depreciation allowances
New equity	new share issues
Bonds	short-term bonds and long-term bonds. New bonds include convertible bond and stock warrants
Short-term loans	short-term loans from banking institutions
Long-term loans	long-term loans from banking institutions plus foreign loans and other long-term loans
Trade credit	short-term and long-term payables plus deferred liabilities
Other	other accounts payables and accrued payables and other current liabilities

Table A.3.6 Manufacturing flow of funds data: net sources

Sources	**Contents and Notes**
Retentions	same as gross figure
Securities	gross new equity and bonds minus financial investment in equities and bonds and other assets. Other asset includes long-term loans receivables, long-term loans to stockholders,

	employees and affiliated companies, leasehold rights and telephone rights etc.
Short-term loans	gross minus cash and other deposits
Long-term loans	same as gross figure
Trade credit	gross minus short-term and long-term receivables and deferred assets
Other	gross minus other accounts receivable and accrued receivables and other current assets

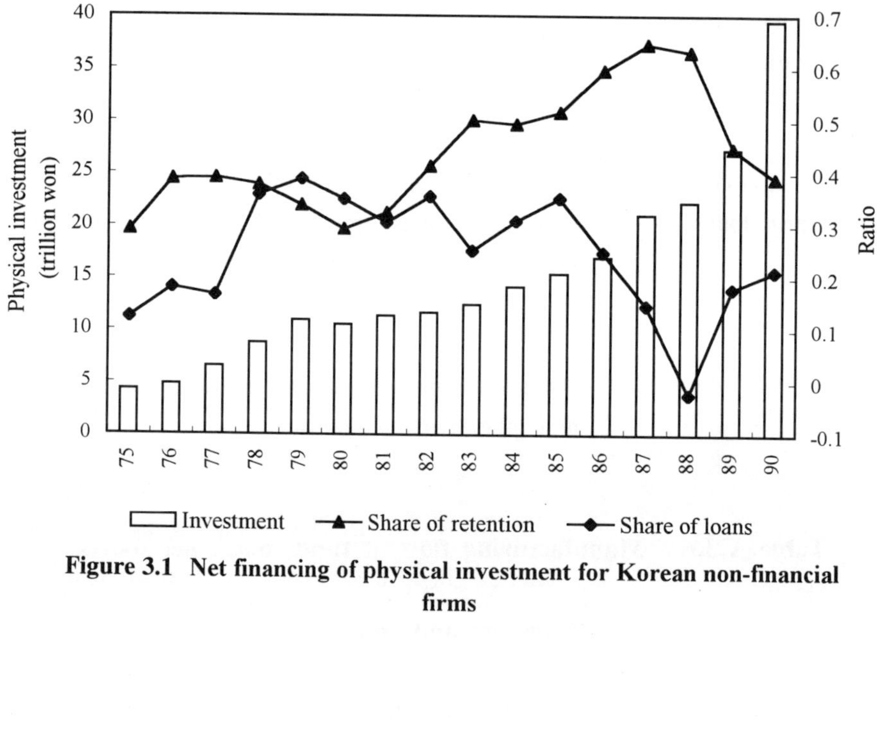

Figure 3.1 Net financing of physical investment for Korean non-financial firms

Notes

1. Mayer (1990) points out that while in the UK the revaluation of assets in company accounts is quite common, in Japan and the US it is a rare practice. In Germany asset revaluation is forbidden by law. In Korea, if the inflation rate is above a certain level, firms are allowed to revalue assets and this commonly occurs.
2. Prowse (1990) points out that while most Japanese firms use double-declining balance methods for depreciation, US firms predominantly use straight-line methods. This difference is expected to introduce some inconsistencies between the two countries' total asset figures, and thus the gearing ratios.
3. Singh and Hamid (1992) use a stock-based approach to examine the pattern of corporate finance in developing countries.
4. We cannot calculate the net contribution of new equity accurately for one of the data sets we use in this chapter because a separate figure for financial investment in equities is not available. This data limitation will be discussed further in section 3.3.
5. Our method for the weighted average is: $\sum_{t=1975}^{1990} i_t^j \frac{P_K}{P_t} / \sum_{t=1975}^{1990} I_t \frac{P_K}{P_t}$

   where i_t^j denotes the amount of finance of type j in year t (measured in current prices in year t), I_t denotes total finance in year t (that is, the sum of all the different types of finance in year t), P_t denotes the price index in year t and year K is the base year, 1985. The capital goods price index is obtained from the Bank of Korea.
6. In this chapter, we use aggregated company accounts data for manufacturing firms in Korea. In the following chapter we will use individual company accounts for a sample of large Korean corporations.
7. In the Korean case, the company accounts of a company cover the operations of a foreign branch of this company, but not those of a foreign subsidiary which will have its own company accounts.

8. Korea can be classified as having a 'two book' accounting system, as in the US and UK. Accounts used for tax calculations may contain different information (e.g.depreciation) from that reported in published company accounts. In the Financial Statement Analysis, although the sample has been taken from firms which report corporate tax data to the Tax Bureau, the company accounts used by the Bank are the published company accounts. For a detailed discussion of this issue, see Cummins, Harris and Hassett (1994).
9. The number of manufacturing firms in the sample has increased as follows:

year	1980	1983	1986	1989
number of firms	1267	1345	1586	2081

Sources: The Bank of Korea, Financial Statement Analysis, various issues.

10. Internally generated funds includes both retained profits and depreciation provisions.
11. Corbett and Jenkinson (1994) pointed out that during the 1970s Japanese firms used more bank finance when internal funding was low, giving a distinct negative correlation between the two series, but during the 1980s this relationship has loosened and the use of bank finance has not been as closely related to the level of 'need' indicated by internal finance. In our data set, the negative correlation between internal finance and loan financing remains pronounced throughout the 1980s.
12. We compare the results for the manufacturing flow of funds data with the unweighted average figures for the aggregate flow of funds data, presented in Appendix 3.2.
13. Note that financial investment in shares and bonds cannot be separated in our manufacturing flow of funds data and consequently only the net share of finance from both types of securities can be reported.

14. Corbett and Jenkinson (1994) note that the negative figure for equity financing in the US has resulted from netting out intra-sector purchases and sales of equity (of the corporate sector by the corporate sector), which renders making the comparison of this figure with that in the other countries unreasonable.
15. Singh and Hamid (1992) reached similar conclusion from a stock-based analysis of corporate finance, using company accounts data for the top 50 companies in nine developing countries for the period 1980-1988, including Korea. First, the largest corporations in these developing countries use a lower share of internal funds than do corporations in developed countries. Second, these corporations use a higher share of new equity financing than corporations in developed countries. Singh (1995) assesses the robustness of results from Singh and Hamid (1992) by increasing the size of the samples and by including one more developing country and also seeks to compare its results with Mayer (1988,1990) results. Cobham and Subramaniam (1995) also investigated the patterns of investment finance of the Indian corporate sector from sectoral and firm-level data using Mayer-type methodology and compared their results with the finding from Singh and Hamid (1995). They argued that the case of India can be broadly compared to 'low' internal finance countries such as France and Italy, which have small-scale stock market and little market for corporate control.
16. Mayer (1988) obtained the same finding for Japan in his international comparison. He argued that the equity market in Japan has made a positive contribution to financing its domestic capital formation as the infrequency of takeovers has made net repurchases of shares much smaller.
17. This exposition is adopted from Corbett and Jenkinson (1994).

4 The pattern of investment finance in Korea: Evidence from company accounts data

4.1 Introduction

The main objective of this chapter is to investigate the pattern of investment finance for large Korean corporations, using company accounts data. This also allows us to consider the representativeness of this sample compared to the aggregate data used in Chapter 3. An econometric study of investment using this sample of companies will be presented in Chapter 6.

The first part of this chapter will explain how the company accounts data has been collected and analysed, although the detailed definition of each variable will be provided in Appendix 4.1. Subsequently we will describe the pattern of funding corporate investment using this sample. In this process the sample will be divided according to interesting structural features of the Korean corporate sector, and in particular according to whether companies are members of a Chaebol group. This part can be viewed as a sequel to Chapter 3, which analysed the same issues using aggregate data. The aggregate data and our firm-level accounting data are different in their coverage and representativeness, and in the precise definition of each of the sources of finance. In the final section, we will compare the main findings with our results using aggregate data in Chapter 3, and draw some conclusions that will guide our econometric study of investment behaviour.

4.2 Description of the sample

Firm-level company accounts data has several advantages, despite the basic problem that accounting information does not always correspond directly to economically interesting concepts. As we mentioned in Chapter 3, the prime advantage of using company accounts over aggregate flow of funds data is in the precise nature and internal consistency of the former (see Mayer 1990), whereas the latter data is likely to be imprecise because it is collected from various sources. In addition, we can consider interesting sub-samples of company data, such as firms who belong to Chaebol groups.

The firm-level company accounts data used in this thesis was compiled by Korea Investors Service, a credit rating agency in Korea, based on the reported company accounts[1] and their own questionnaires. The database originally included not only listed companies but also unlisted companies and registered companies totalling 21,670 firms as of the end of 1991. However the data we had access to only includes firms which were listed on the Korea Stock Exchange (KSE) as of the end of 1991, and the maximum data period is from 1982 to 1991. The data does not only contain observations on quoted firms, but includes earlier observations when these firms were not quoted. In fact, each firm may have observations prior to its listing in the Stock Exchange. The rule of thumb of making the database in Korea Investors Service was to keep 5 years of data prior to the listing if this was available. We keep this additional information in our sample because it gives us more data points for analysis. We will use the sub-set of strictly stock market listed observations when we estimate stock market-related models such as the Q model in Chapter 6, but unless otherwise specified we will keep as many observations as possible.

The data includes only non-financial firms which as mentioned above have been listed on KSE at the end of 1991. There are also some firms which were listed previously but do not exist any longer for reasons such as bankruptcy. In that case, the firm remains in the data set for 5 years. Financial companies were excluded from the sample because their physical investment behaviour is unlikely to be directly comparable to that of non-financial firms. Lastly, if firms have changed the month in which their accounting year ended, we retained the longest sequence of consecutive years in our sample. We also applied the same procedure if there were missing items for a firm, or missing years.

Table 4.1 outlines the distribution of annual observations and the corresponding number of companies, both for the whole sample and for manufacturing firms. About 70 % of the sample firms have 10 observations from 1982 to 1991. In this chapter we will focus on this balanced sub-sample of the data, so that changes in the pattern of investment finance over time are not being driven by changes in the composition of the sample.

The data set has the full characteristics of a panel data set in that it covers several years for each firm and has a large number of cross-sectional data points. Each firm has about 200 accounting items from the four major accounting statements: balance sheet, income statement, statement of appropriation of retained earnings and flow of funds statement.

In organising the data set, two important steps have been taken. First, the subset of items of interest for our analysis was selected from the total accounting items available. Secondly, additional variables were merged with the selected accounting variables. These additional variables include industry code, group affiliation code, export ratio, date of establishment, date of stock market listing, stock price at the end of the accounting year, number of shares outstanding, number of employees, and year and month of the most recent balance sheet revaluation for each firm. Among these variables, the share price and the number of shares outstanding have been collected from a different source, Daewoo Securities. Matching this stock price information to the accounts data was laborious because the company codes used by Daewoo Securities were different from those used by KIS. Moreover, the stock price information was not available in a computerised format. We had to collect these figures manually from the 'Handbook of Korean listed companies' published annually by Daewoo Securities in Korea. Further details of these additional variables are presented in Appendix 4.1.

For the analysis of this chapter, we also converted the reported flow of funds statement from a working capital basis to a cash flow basis. These two different approaches to the flow of funds statement use different concepts of 'funds'. In the former case (working capital basis), 'funds' are interpreted as an ongoing pool of funds, working capital, which reflects the difference between changes in current assets and current liabilities. The concept of 'working capital' has developed on an accrual basis, meaning that expenses are matched with sales, rather than cash payments being matched with cash receipts. In the second concept (cash flow basis), funds are interpreted as 'cash and its equivalents', that every item in the account is recorded as an inflow or outflow of cash.[2] In Korea, firms have only been required to report a cash flow based financing table alongside the traditional working capital based financing table since 1994. However, by applying the conversion formulae set out by Korea Investors Service (1992), we can derive estimates of the sources and uses of funds on a cash flow basis. This cash flow basis was considered to be more appropriate for our study of investment finance. By converting the format of the flow of funds statement in this way, we lost the 1982 data and are left with 9 observations from 1983-1991.

In Table 4.2 we divide our total sample of manufacturing firms according to certain criteria derived from the discussion of Korean corporate structure in Chapter 2. Size of the firm, group affiliation, age and export-orientedness were our principal concerns. If the average annual number of employees throughout the period is more than 1000, the firm is here classified as a large firm. A firm is considered as an affiliate of a Chaebol group if the firm belongs to one of the 50 largest Chaebol groups; is regarded as an old firm if it was already established as of 1960; and is classed as an export firm if its ratio of exports to total sales exceeds 30%.

We can observe some inter-relationships between these sample separation criteria. If we first look at the relationship between size and group affiliation, 69 % of group firms are large firms and 75 % of non-group firms are small and medium firms. Similarly, 59 % of large firms are affiliated to a group, while 82 % of small and medium-sized firms are non-group firms. These figures suggest that size and group-affiliation have a close interaction with each other. Secondly, we consider the relationship between age and these size and group characteristics. 43 % of large firms and 39 % of group firms were established before 1960, whilst 74 % of small and medium-sized firms and 70 % of non-group firms began to operate after 1960. Non-group firms and small firms certainly have a tendency to be young firms, while for large firms and group firms we observe a rather more even distribution between young and old firms. We also observe that while young firms tend to be small and not affiliated to groups, old firms are quite evenly divided by size and groups characteristics. This partly reflects the fact that a high proportion of listed member companies of Chaebol groups have been established after 1960, even though the flagship general trading companies of these groups have mostly existed from well before 1960.

Lastly, we observe that export-orientedness is not found to have a close relationship with size or group affiliation. Considering the fact that export activities have been central to the development of Chaebol groups, this may appear surprising. But as Choi and Cho (1987) have pointed out, in most Chaebol groups, most of the export activities are carried out through the flagship trading company at the heart of the group, even if the products are manufactured by the member companies. These exports are recorded in the accounts of the flagship company. As our company accounts is unconsolidated accounts, this practice underestimates the extent to which group member companies are actually producing for export markets.

4.3 The pattern of finance in large Korean corporations

In this section, we use the same methodologies as in the analysis of aggregate flow of funds data in the previous chapter: the flow concepts of sources of finances are calculated on a gross and net basis. As we reviewed in section 3.2 of Chapter 3, gross sources of finance are measured as a proportion of total gross sources and net sources of finance as a proportion of physical investment. We calculated the weighted average[3] shares of gross and net sources of finance over the period 1983-1991 and over two sub-periods, 1983-1987 and 1988-1991, for a balanced panel of 420 firms (319 manufacturing firms). By comparing the results for these sub-periods, we investigate whether significant changes in the financing patterns of Korean firms occurred during our sample period.

We report the shares of seven separate sources of finance: internal funds, new equity issues, bonds, short-term loans,[4] long-term loans, trade credit and other sources. It should be noted that in our company flow of funds accounts, separate figures for financial investment in equity and bonds are not available, and therefore the net shares of finance from new equity and bonds could not be calculated separately. Instead, we report the share of securities on a net basis. However, unlike the aggregate manufacturing accounts data used in Chapter 3, we can distinguish financial investment in securities from other financial investment, so that a more accurate measure of the net contribution of securities finance can be estimated.

Major observations for the total sample and the manufacturing sample

Tables 4.3 and 4.4 present gross and net sources of finance for all firms in the sample and for all manufacturing firms. The gross and net figures in the two tables do not show very large differences in financing patterns between these two different samples but a few points are worth mentioning before we concentrate on the results for the manufacturing sample.

First, the contribution of internally generated funds is larger for the manufacturing sample than for the total sample, on both the gross and net basis. Note that on the net basis, the share of internal funds is not very different between the two samples in the first sub-period, but in the second sub-period the gap widens.

Second, the manufacturing firms use a lower share of loans, especially long-term loans, than the total sample. However this difference is dominated by the pattern in the first sub-period, and did not occur in the later period 1988-1991.

Third, it is also observed that the pattern of finance for manufacturing firms was more stable over time than for total sample. Particularly in the

total sample, the share of finance from the trade credit and long-term loans displayed an abrupt change between the two sub-periods.

With these comparisons in mind, we now focus on the results from the manufacturing sample. A number of observations emerge from Table 4.4. First, of these seven categories of finance, internal funds made the biggest contribution on both the gross and net basis. This highest contribution from retentions was the typical result from the analysis of other financial systems, as pointed out in Mayer (1988,1990) and Corbett and Jenkinson (1994). As we discussed in Chapter 3, the share of retentions in Korea is actually much lower than in most other developed countries.

Second, the share of finance from equity and bond markets increased considerably as we move across the sub-periods. The net share of securities increased from 23.9 % in 1983-1987 to 41.4 % in 1988-1991. The sharp increase in finance from new equity issues may reflect the rapid growth of the Korean stock market in the latter half of the 1980s.

Considering the underdevelopment of Korean financial markets, the figure for bond financing (on a gross basis) is surprisingly high, especially in the later sub-period. This unusually high figure for bond financing is probably related to the development of the Korean government's financial policy in the 1980s. The Korean government strongly promoted the corporate bond market and allowed corporate bond yields to rise above bank deposit rates in the early 1980s (see Cho 1989). We also note that bond finance in Korea can be regarded as an extended form of long-term bank finance, because the bonds were usually sold with the guarantee of a commercial bank and the typical maturity of these bonds is 2-3 years. Therefore it may be argued that the character of the Korean bond market cannot be interpreted as purely a 'market' source of finance, as is the case for more developed countries, and this high figure for bond financing in the period does not automatically suggests the expansion of market sources of finance.

Third, finance from loans remains one of the major sources of finance in Korea, although its share did decline somewhat in the course of the 1980s. Across the sub-periods, the net share of short-term loans slightly increases, but the net share of long-term loans declines. This may be an indication that the declining banking sector in Korea has lost some of its previous dominance as a provider of long-term finance, which was vital in the earlier stages of economic development. At the same time, although it is a bit marginal, the slightly increasing net share of short-term loans could be a reflection of a change in the environment, in which the Korean banks found it more difficult to require 'compensating balances' from the borrower, as they faced increasing competition from other financial institutions.

Fourth, trade credit made a distinctly negative contribution to net finance over the entire period, meaning that the firms in our sample were net lenders to other traders. Unlike the total sample, in which trade credit displayed a volatile pattern between sub-periods, the manufacturing firms showed a quite stable share of trade credit.

Comparison with evidence from manufacturing flow of funds data

The financing pattern of manufacturing firms in our company accounts sample may be compared to the corresponding results for the aggregated manufacturing sector in Chapter 3. However, it should be made clear that this comparison between the two results can only be done with qualifications, for the following reasons.

First of all, while in Chapter 3 we used the representative sample of accounts data for manufacturing firms collected by the Bank of Korea, the analysis in this chapter is based on our sample of large manufacturing corporations, all of which were listed on the KSE by the end of 1991. Note that of the 319 companies in our sample, 275 companies are 'large' by the criteria employed in Chapter 3, as will be discussed again in the next section.[5] Note also that in this chapter the sample covers the period 1983-1991 only. These differences in the composition of the samples used in each chapter should be considered in comparing the results from the manufacturing sector in each chapter.

Second, the individual company accounts used here allowed us to separate financial investment in securities from other financial investment, as detailed in Appendix 4.2, whereas in Chapter 3 we could not distinguish between them. Recall that the resulting net share of securities reported in Chapter 3 is likely to be underestimated, while this is not the case here. To make the results more comparable, however, we can re-compute the net share of securities in the company accounts sample of this chapter on the same basis that had to be used in Chapter 3.

Third, we used different methods to calculate the share of finance in each chapter. While in Chapter 3 we had to use the unweighted average method to calculate the gross and net shares of finance, in this chapter we calculate the figures on the weighted average basis. However in Chapter 3 it was shown that taking weighted or unweighted averages over years did not have a major impact on the results.

By comparing the manufacturing company sample in this chapter with the whole manufacturing sector in Chapter 3, we can consider how representative our manufacturing sample is. We first compare the results for our sample of companies in 1983-1991 with results for the whole manufacturing sector from Chapter 3, over both 1975-1990 and 1985-1990. On the gross basis, while the share of internal funds is quite similar between the two samples, the share of securities is much higher in our company sample, and the share of loans is lower. It should be noted that the difference in the share of securities mostly comes from the share of bonds. The net shares of finance also show a similar pattern.[6] If we compare the average shares of finance for our manufacturing company sample with the results for the manufacturing sector for the period

1985-1990, which is likely to be more appropriate, we observe a similar pattern, although our sample firms also use a lower share of internal finance in this period. In summary, we observe that the manufacturing sample in this chapter relied more on bonds and less on loans than the manufacturing sector as a whole. This is consistent with the observation that larger firms tend to use more bonds and less loans.

Sub-samples by group affiliation

Having reviewed the typical features of Korean corporate finance using these total samples, we can now look at how the financing pattern differs for different sub-samples of firms, benefiting from the panel structure of our data. We divide the total manufacturing sample into sub-samples according to the various selection criteria detailed above: group affiliation, size, export ratio, age and industry classification.

Tables 4.5 and 4.6 present the gross and net proportions of each financing source for group-affiliated firms and non-group firms respectively. First we will document the main observations from each table and point out the similarities and differences between these two sub-samples.

For group firms, the average figure for each source of finance is quite similar to the results for our total manufacturing sample in Table 4.4. This observation is not surprising because these figures are weighted averages and the share of group firms is much bigger than that of non-group firms in either total sources of finance or total physical investment.[7] We can also observe similar trends between the two sub-periods. In Table 4.5, the shares of new equity and bonds have increased, and the shares of retentions and long-term loans have decreased over the period, as was the case in Table 4.4.

More interestingly, the share of financing sources for non-group firms is different from the results for group-affiliated firms on the following points.

First, non-group firms used a bigger share of internal funds than group firms on average over the period, although the share of internal funds declined for both group and non-group firms. This difference is especially clear on the net basis.

Second, the share of long-term loans and bonds is higher for group firms, as is the net share of securities finance. However, it is interesting to note that across the sub-periods, the net share of long-term loans declines for group firms but not for non-group firms.

Despite such differences in the shares of different sources of finance between group and non-group firms, there are some similar trends over time. For both sub-samples there is a decline in the share of internal funds, matched by an increase in the share of new equity and bonds. The shares of short-term loans and new equity show similar movements, although for non-group firm the gross share of new equity finance increases by a greater proportion than for group firms.

To summarize, the major differences are that non-group firms rely more on internal finance, and less on long-term loans and securities than do group firms.

Sub-samples by size

Tables 4.7 and 4.8 show the gross and net sources of finance of large firms and small and medium-sized firms. The total sample was divided according to the average number of employees over the period. If this was more than 1000, the firm was classified as large. It should be remembered that the cut-off point for classifying firms according to size in the aggregate manufacturing flow of funds data used in Chapter 3 was 300 employees, so that many of the companies classified as 'small and medium-sized' in this analysis would have been classified as 'large' in the aggregate statistics.[8]

This classification has brought about quite similar observations on the financing patterns as between group and non-group firms. That is, small and medium-sized firms depend more on retentions and less on long-term borrowing than do large firms.

A few further points should be noted, however. First, although the share of internal funds is bigger for small and medium-sized firms than for large firms on average, the difference between these two sub-samples is not so great as between group firms and non-group firms. Moreover, this difference is concentrated in the first sub-period 1983-1987 on both the gross and net basis, and the shares of internal funds for both larger and smaller firms converged to similar level in the second sub-period.

Second, for securities as a whole the increase is more pronounced for larger firms. It appears that this observation is mainly due to the big increase in the share of bonds for larger firms. Note that the percentage increase in the gross share of new equity is greater for smaller firms.

Third, we observe different changes over time in the maturity of loans between these two sub-samples. On the gross basis, while the share of short-term loans does not show any noticeable change across the sub-periods for either sub-sample, long-term loans gain in importance for small and medium-sized firms and decline in importance for large firms. However, the change of debt maturity is observed more clearly on the net basis. Small firms rely more on short-term loans in the first sub-period, but use more long-term loans in the second sub-period. Interestingly, in the second sub-period, the maturity structure of small and medium-sized firms converges to that of large firms.

Comparing these results with those for 'large' and 'small' firms in the manufacturing sector analysis of Chapter 3 is not possible because the size classification between the two data sets is different. Most of the manufacturing firms studied in this chapter are 'large' in the sense of Chapter 3.

Sub-samples by export ratio

Tables 4.9 and 4.10 present the gross and net sources of finance for export and domestic firms. The dividing criteria for these sub-samples is whether the ratio of exports to total sales is over 30 %. A few interesting observations emerge from the comparison of financing patterns between export firms and domestic firms.

The first point is that domestic firms rely less on internal funds and use more finance from new equity and bonds, proportionately, than do export firms. This difference in the shares of equity and bond financing on both the gross and net basis diminishes in the second sub-period. Thus there was some convergence between these two sub-samples in their shares of equity and bond financing.

Second, there is a similar change of debt maturity as we observed in early this section. On the net basis, while for export firms the share of short-term loans increased and the share of long-term decreased across the two sub-periods, the opposite was true for domestic firms. Again this may reflect the change of policy environment in which the government has distanced itself from assisting large and export firms through privileged access to long-term loans, and the effect of this financial liberalisation is realised in the latter half of the 1980s.

Third, the net share of finance from trade credit shows an opposite movement between these two sub-samples. The negative contribution of trade credit becomes more pronounced in the second sub-period for export firms. In other words, the export firms increased their net lending to other firms in this second period. In contrast, across these sub-periods the trade credit figures for domestic firms show a declining net lending position.

To sum up, export firms were more reliant on internal finance and less reliant on equity and bond financing. The structure of debt maturity converged between export firms and domestic firms.

In Chapter 3, we did not find these differences between export and domestic firms. This may be partly due to the difference in sample periods. Moreover, in comparing these results, it should be noted that while in Chapter 3, we divided a representative sample of manufacturing firms into export and domestic sectors, in this chapter we divided a sample of large corporations into those categories. This difference in the size of firms in the two samples is coupled with the fact that the exports of member companies of Chaebol groups are generally channelled through the flagship company, called the General Trading Company, of the group and consequently some misclassification is likely to occur. This misclassification problem is likely to have a less severe impact on sample used in Chapter 3, since a smaller proportion of companies will belong to Chaebol groups.

Sub-samples by age

Tables 4.11 and 4.12 present the results using sub-samples divided by age. If the firm was established as of 1960, it is classed as old; and if established after 1960, it is regarded as young.

In this classification, we note that young firms used a higher share of internal funds, although the difference is not very large, especially in the second sub-period. Young firms also used a lower share of both equity and bond financing compared to old firms, which is consistent with the common observation that older firms are larger and less risky, and have established reputations, which makes it easier for them to issue securities.

In contrast, younger firms used, in proportionate terms, a higher share of finance from loans, especially on the net basis. Over time, old firms tended to switch from long-term loans to new equity and bonds, whilst the share of long-term loans increased for younger firms.

Sub-samples by industry classification

In Tables 4.13 and 4.14, we present the results when we divide the total sample by whether the firm operates in a heavy or light industry. The industries classified as heavy and light are detailed in Appendix 4.1. We point out some important differences between these two samples.

First, light-industry firms used a distinctly higher share of internal funds, although this difference was much smaller in the second sub-period. Light-industry firms used a lower share of finance from securities (especially new equity) and a lower share of finance from long-term loans, especially in the first sub-period.

Second, light-industry firms were net trade debtors, whereas heavy-industry firms were net trade creditors over this period.

Third, while for heavy industry firms the share of short-term and long-term loans were both decreasing over the sub-periods, the share of loans for light- industry firms was increasing, although this increase was concentrated in short-term loans.

The first point above was also observed in the results for heavy and light industry firms in Chapter 3. In Table 3.8 of Chapter 3, we also observed that light-industry firms used a slightly higher share of internal funds and used a distinctly lower share of securities. If we again compute the net share of securities according to the definition used in Chapter 3, the net share of securities is 29.2 % for heavy-industry firms and 23.5 % for light-industry firms. These figures are again much higher than the corresponding figures in Chapter 3, but show a similar pattern between these two sub-samples.

The difference in the net shares of trade credit between heavy and light industries was not found in the analysis of Chapter 3, which may again reflect differences in the size composition of firms in our sample.

4.4 Summary and conclusions

In this chapter, we first described the structure of our Korean company accounts data and then examined the financing patterns of Korean companies.

We investigated not only the total samples of companies and of manufacturing companies, but also various sub-samples of manufacturing companies divided according to structural features of Korean corporations.

The results from our analysis of company accounts flow of funds data can be summarised as follows. First, internal funds and loans remain major sources of finance, while the share of new equity and bond financing was increasing in importance in the course of our data period (1983-1991). The nature of bond financing in Korea being different from that in more developed bond markets, the high figure for bond financing should be interpreted with care. The contribution of loans was declining over the period. This trend reflects the change in the Korean government's financial policy in the 1980s, so that the previously dominant position of banks as a provider of finance was encroached by the expansion of the stock market and the bond market.

Second, dividing the sample by criteria such as group affiliation, size and export ratio showed how the financing pattern differs between these sub-samples. Group affiliation and size were shown to have a similar effect on corporate financing patterns. Group firms tend to use significantly more long-term external finance and less internal finance than non-group firms. The same is true for large firms compared to small and medium-sized firms. We also observe that differences in financing patterns among our other sub-samples were not as consistent and pronounced as between the group and size classifications.

Third, it is dangerous to attach too much importance to results from dividing our sample period into two, as these sub-periods are very short. Nonetheless, it is interesting to observe some changes which appear to be consistent with the background of financial deregulation. Most importantly, in the later sub-period compared with the earlier sub-period, the non-group firms and smaller firms tended to increase their share of long-term finance and new equity finance more sharply than the group firms and larger firms. However, we should observe this increase in the share of new equity finance with some qualification because this data set includes not only observations when firms were listed but also observations prior to listing on the KSE. Particularly for non-group and smaller firms, there is the possibility that we underestimate the proportion of finance from new equity in the first half of the 1980s.

However, these findings do not establish any particular conclusions about the relationship between financial factors and the investment spending of Korean corporations. We cannot conclude that the investment spending of a certain group of firms is more affected by financial constraints than another group of firms on the basis of these observed patterns of financing. This issue will be investigated more directly by an econometric analysis in Chapter 6. In Chapter 5 we will first review the related literatures on which this analysis draws.

Table 4.1 Number of observations per firm

	Number of firms	
Number of observations[9]	Whole sample	Manufacturing firms
3	3	2
4	4	2
5	14	12
6	33	28
7	36	32
8	35	26
9	53	44
10	420	319
total	598	465

Table 4.2 Composition of the sample

Large firms	189	Group	111	Old	82	Export	94
		Non-G	78	Young	107	Dom	95
Small firms	276	Group	48	Old	71	Export	109
		Non-G	228	Young	205	Dom	167
Group firms	159	Large	111	Old	62	Export	61
		Small	48	Young	97	Dom	98
Non-group firms	306	Large	77	Old	91	Export	142
		Small	229	Young	215	Dom	164
Old firms	153	Large	82	Group	62	Export	49
		Small	71	Non-G	91	Dom	104
Young firms	312	Large	107	Group	97	Export	154
		Small	205	Non-G	215	Dom	158
Export firms	203	Large	94	Group	61	Old	49
		Small	109	Non-G	142	Young	154
Domestic firms	262	Large	95	Group	98	Old	104
		Small	167	Non-G	164	Young	158

Notes:

Large firm: average number of employees ≥ 1000
Small firm: average number of employees < 1000
Group firm: affiliated to one of the 50 largest Chaebol groups
Non-group firm: not so affiliated
Old firm: established before 1960
Young firm: established after 1960
Export firm: ratio of exports to total sales ≥ 30 %
Domestic firm: ratio of exports to total sales < 30 %

Table 4.3 Sources of finance for the total sample (420 firms)

Gross sources

	internal funds	new equity	bonds	short loans	long loans	trade credit	other
83-91	29.1	9.8	16.3	12.3	10.2	17.8	4.7
83-87	35.0	6.7	12.3	12.3	16.9	13.8	2.9
88-91	26.1	11.2	18.2	12.3	6.8	19.7	5.6
Net sources							
83-91	55.5	37.4		9.6	19.4	-7.0	-14.9
83-87	65.8	27.3		7.6	31.8	-15.2	-17.3
88-91	50.3	42.6		10.5	13.1	-2.8	-13.7

Source: KIS line company accounts.

Note: short-term loans if the maturity is less than 1 year and long-term loans otherwise. This note applies to Tables 4.3-4.14.

Table 4.4 Sources of finance for all manufacturing firms (319 firms)

Gross sources

	internal funds	new equity	bonds	short loans	long loans	trade credit	other
83-91	33.6	9.6	16.8	12.3	8.9	14.8	4.0
83-87	39.9	7.3	11.5	12.4	10.7	14.2	4.0
88-91	30.5	10.7	19.4	12.2	8.1	15.0	4.0
Net sources							
83-91	59.2	35.5		8.8	15.8	-7.2	-12.0
83-87	67.2	23.9		7.8	18.0	-8.7	-8.2
88-91	55.1	41.4		9.4	14.6	-6.4	-14.0

Table 4.5 Sources of finance for group-affiliated firms (135 firms)

Gross sources	internal funds	new equity	bonds	short loans	long loans	trade credit	other
83-91	32.5	9.6	17.2	12.1	9.4	15.0	4.3
83-87	38.1	7.6	11.8	12.5	11.5	13.9	4.6
88-91	29.9	10.5	19.7	12.0	8.4	15.4	4.1
Net sources							
83-91	56.6	36.1		9.1	16.3	-6.7	-11.5
83-87	64.1	24.4		8.1	19.3	-8.7	-7.1
88-91	53.1	41.8		9.6	14.9	-5.8	-13.6

Table 4.6 Sources of finance for non-group affiliated firms (184 firms)

Gross sources	internal funds	new equity	bonds	short loans	long loans	trade credit	other
83-91	39.5	9.3	14.8	13.2	6.7	13.7	2.7
83-87	47.2	5.8	10.7	12.1	7.3	15.4	1.6
88-91	34.3	11.7	17.6	14.0	6.3	12.6	3.5
Net sources							
83-91	74.1	31.3		7.3	12.6	-10.0	-15.2
83-87	80.4	22.6		6.4	12.5	-8.8	-13.1
88-91	69.0	38.2		8.0	12.7	-11.0	-16.9

Table 4.7 Sources of finance for large firms (161 firms)

Gross sources

	internal funds	new equity	bonds	short loans	long loans	trade credit	other
83-91	33.1	9.2	17.2	12.2	9.2	14.9	4.3
83-87	38.5	7.4	11.2	12.2	11.6	14.4	4.6
88-91	30.4	10.1	20.1	12.2	8.0	15.1	4.1
Net sources							
83-91	58.4	35.2		8.8	16.2	-7.1	-11.4
83-87	64.4	23.6		6.7	19.4	-7.4	-6.5
88-91	55.2	41.4		9.9	14.5	-6.9	-14.0

Table 4.8 Sources of finance for small and medium-sized firms (158 firms)

Gross sources

	internal funds	new equity	bonds	short loans	long loans	trade credit	other
83-91	37.1	11.9	14.4	12.8	7.6	14.0	2.2
83-87	48.3	6.5	13.5	13.7	4.8	13.1	0.2
88-91	31.5	14.7	14.8	12.3	9.0	14.5	3.2
Net sources							
83-91	64.7	36.8		9.3	13.2	-8.0	-15.9
83-87	86.4	27.2		15.2	8.5	-17.2	-20.1
88-91	54.1	41.5		6.4	15.4	-3.5	-13.9

Table 4.9 Sources of finance for export firms (128 firms)

Gross sources	internal funds	new equity	bonds	short loans	long loans	trade credit	other
83-91	36.1	8.1	16.0	11.6	9.4	14.8	4.0
83-87	40.0	5.7	8.7	10.9	14.5	17.2	3.0
88-91	34.1	9.4	19.9	11.9	6.7	13.5	4.5
Net sources							
83-91	62.5	30.3		8.6	16.2	-7.2	-10.3
83-87	65.0	17.5		5.3	23.5	-2.0	-9.3
88-91	61.1	37.6		10.5	12.0	-10.3	-11.0

Table 4.10 Sources of finance for domestic firms (191 firms)

Gross sources	internal funds	new equity	bonds	short loans	long loans	trade credit	other
83-91	30.9	11.1	17.6	13.1	8.5	14.8	4.0
83-87	39.7	9.1	14.9	14.2	6.3	10.7	5.1
88-91	27.0	11.9	18.9	12.6	9.5	16.6	3.5
Net sources							
83-91	55.6	41.0		9.1	15.3	-7.2	-13.8
83-87	70.0	32.2		10.9	11.0	-17.1	-7.0
88-91	48.9	45.2		8.3	17.3	-2.5	-17.0

Table 4.11 Sources of finance for old firms (135 firms)

Gross sources

	internal funds	new equity	bonds	short loans	long loans	trade credit	other
83-91	31.6	11.0	16.9	12.3	8.1	16.2	4.0
83-87	34.6	7.8	13.0	10.4	12.7	16.9	4.7
88-91	30.0	12.8	19.1	13.3	5.5	15.8	3.6

Net sources

	internal funds	new equity	bonds	short loans	long loans	trade credit	other
83-91	56.8	39.3		7.6	14.5	-5.6	-12.5
83-87	59.9	28.8		6.4	21.9	-11.0	-6.0
88-91	54.9	45.4		8.4	10.0	-2.5	-16.3

Table 4.12 Sources of finance for young firms (184 firms)

Gross sources

	internal funds	new equity	bonds	short loans	long loans	trade credit	other
83-91	34.9	8.6	16.8	12.3	9.5	13.8	4.0
83-87	44.1	6.8	10.4	14.1	9.1	12.1	3.5
88-91	30.9	9.4	19.6	11.6	9.7	14.6	4.3

Net sources

	internal funds	new equity	bonds	short loans	long loans	trade credit	other
83-91	60.8	32.9		9.6	16.6	-8.2	-11.7
83-87	72.8	20.3		8.8	15.0	-6.9	-9.9
88-91	55.2	38.9		10.0	17.4	-8.9	-12.6

Table 4.13 Sources of finance for heavy-industry firms (213 firms)

Gross sources	internal funds	new equity	bonds	short loans	long loans	trade credit	other
83-91	31.4	10.5	16.9	12.0	9.8	14.9	4.5
83-87	35.7	8.4	12.0	13.4	12.1	14.0	4.4
88-91	29.3	11.5	19.3	11.3	8.7	15.4	4.5
Net sources							
83-91	56.5	38.0		9.2	17.7	-9.6	-11.8
83-87	61.8	26.9		10.6	20.9	-12.6	-7.6
88-91	53.9	43.5		8.6	16.1	-8.2	-13.9

Table 4.14 Sources of finance for light-industry firms (106 firms)

Gross sources	internal funds	new equity	bonds	short loans	long loans	trade credit	other
83-91	41.2	6.3	16.4	13.4	6.0	14.2	2.5
83-87	52.7	3.7	10.2	9.5	6.3	15.0	2.7
88-91	34.9	7.7	19.8	15.6	5.8	13.8	2.3
Net sources							
83-91	67.6	27.4		7.5	9.8	0.3	-12.7
83-87	82.3	15.7		-0.2	9.9	2.2	-9.9
88-91	58.9	34.3		12.1	9.8	-0.7	-14.3

Note: Heavy-industry firms belong to industry groups 5-8 of the manufacturing industries listed in Table A.4.1 of Appendix 4.1.

Appendix 4.1

In constructing our data set, we merged the accounting data with items that are not reported in company accounts, but are used in our empirical analysis. The variables we added to the data set are outlined below.

1) group affiliation: group means a Chaebol group in Korea, as explained in Chapter 2. We selected the fifty largest Chaebol groups (according to total group assets). If a firm is affiliated to one of these, it is classed as a group firm, and not otherwise.
2) number of employees: the number of full-time employees at the end of each year. The average number of employees over the sample period and was used to classify the size of the firm.
3) export ratio: the ratio of the exports to total foreign sales and domestic sales over the last three years of the sample period for each firm.
4) date of establishment: the year and month when a firm was established. This variable is used as a measure of the age of the firm.
5) date of most recent revaluation: if no revaluation is reported within our sample period, we assume that the firm has not revalued its assets since 1982. This variable is used in the calculation of the current-cost capital stock measure in Chapter 6.
6) share price and number of outstanding shares: the average share price in the last month of the accounting year, and the number of outstanding shares at the end of the accounting year, obtained from Daewoo Securities Database.
7) industry code: the industry the firm's business activity falls in, and coded according to the Korea Standard Industry Classification (KSIC), as described in Table A.4.1. These industry codes were obtained from Korea Investors Service.
8) price indices: wholesale price indices for output and investment goods, and land price index for seven major cities in Korea. This

data was obtained from Korea Development Institute and the Bank of Korea, and is described more fully in Chapter 6.

9) year and month of listing: the year and month when a firm was listed on the KSE. This variable was used to define the data set for which share price information is available, which is required for some of the analysis in Chapter 6.

Items (1)-(5) and (9) were obtained from Daewoo Securities (1992).

Table A.4.1 Industry classification and the number of firms by industry

Group	Industry	KSIC code	Number
	Non-manufacturing		101
	Agriculture and fishing	10	4
	Mining	20	3
	Electricity, gas and steam	40	7
	Construction	50	38
	Wholesale and retail trade	60	36
	Transport, storage and communication	70	11
	Recreation	90	2
	Manufacturing	30	319
1	Food and beverage	31	36
2	Textile, wearing apparel and leather	32	48
3	Wood and furniture	33	7
4	Paper,printing and publishing	34	17
5	Chemical, petroleum, coal and plastics	35	86
6	Non-metallic mineral products	36	16
7	Basic metal	37	25
8	Fabricated metal products	38	78
9	Other manufacturing	39	6
	Total		420

Note: Industry groups (5) - (8) are classed as heavy industries, and industry groups (1) - (4) and (9) are classed as light industries.

Appendix 4.2

Table A.4.2 Korean company accounts: gross sources

Sources	Contents and Notes
Internal funds	retained earnings plus depreciation allowances
New equity	new share issues
Bonds	new bond issues minus redemption of bonds: new bonds issues include convertible bonds and stock warrants
Short-term loans	short-term borrowing: includes borrowings to be repaid within one year
Long-term loans	long-term borrowing: includes borrowings repayable within one year
Trade credit	short-term and long-term payables plus deferred liabilities
Other	other current liabilities and fixed liabilities

Table A.4.3 Korean company accounts: net sources

Sources	Contents and Notes
Retentions	same as gross figure
Securities	gross new equity and bonds minus investment in securities: as investment in securities cannot be separated into bonds and equities, only the net share of securities is reported.
Short-term loans	gross minus cash and other deposits
Long-term loans	same as gross figure
Trade credit	gross minus short-term and long-term receivables and deferred assets
Other	gross minus other current assets and other fixed assets

Notes

1. Korea has a so-called 'two book' system. The Korean Corporation Tax law prescribes the accounting principles to be used in determining taxable income, and they can differ from generally accepted accounting principles (GAAP) in some areas such as inventory valuation, depreciation, and bad debt reserves. But here we use commercial accounts, not fiscal (tax) accounts. For a discussion of 'one book' and 'two book' accounting systems, see Cummins, Harris and Hassett (1994).
2. For more detail on the conceptual difference between two accounts, see Taylor and Underwood (1987) and Nam (1988).
3. Our company analysis reports weighted averages in two senses: the weighted average across the sample companies in each year; and the weighted average across years.
4. The maturity of short-term loans does not exceed one year.
5. Recall that in Chapter 3 the companies are classed as large if the number of full-time employees is more than 300.
6. We cannot make an exact comparison on the net basis because as mentioned above other financial investment was netted off against gross securities finance in Chapter 3, as well as financial investment in securities, while this was not the case in this chapter. If we recalculate the net share of securities for our sample on the same basis used in Chapter 3, the net share of securities for our sample of manufacturing firms falls from 35.5 % to 24 %. This is still considerably higher than the figure of 8.3 % for the manufacturing sector as a whole in Chapter 3.
7. In terms of total sources of funds, group firms account for 84.36 % of the whole manufacturing sample. In terms of total investment, group firms account for 84 % of the sample.
8. The number of firms which have fewer than 300 employees in our sample of company accounts is just 44, which is too small to do any meaningful analysis of 'small' firms with the sample of company accounts.

9. Firms with less than 5 observations may have resulted from the elimination of missing values or misplaced observations from the sample, as described in the text.

5 Corporate investment models and financial constraints: A survey

5.1 Introduction

In this chapter, we will focus on the theoretical framework of the investment models to be used in the following econometric analysis, and review the econometric evidence from previous studies. In section 5.2, the main features of the investment models used in Chapter 6 will be discussed, and in section 5.3 we will examine how financial factors could affect investment decisions. This will include a discussion of the implications of the hierarchy of finance model, and how such a financing hierarchy may have operated in the context of Korea. In section 5.4 we will review the findings of existing microeconometric studies of company investment using panel data. In particular, we will compare the results from developed countries such as the US, UK and Japan with the results from developing countries. Studies using company accounts data for developing countries with more repressed financial system have only recently begun to appear, but will potentially produce valuable results. In this section, research using data from Indonesia, Ecuador and Korea will be discussed.

5.2 Alternative investment models

While empirical investment models have developed extensively over the last forty years, the main models can be classed into two principal categories. One comprises the static neoclassical models and the other comprises the dynamic adjustment cost models.

Although investment has long been recognized as an important and volatile component of national income and a source of furthering economic growth, it was after the discussion in Keynes (1936) that economists stepped up their efforts to test empirically the factors that influence investment behaviour. Before Keynes, the so called classical economists viewed investment as being determined in a rather mechanistic way; the investment level was determined when the interest rate or marginal cost of capital equalled the marginal product of capital. They maintained that the interest rate was the medium through which investment was equated with savings. Even if Keynes also argued that the investment rate was determined at the level where the marginal efficiency of capital equalled the interest rate, he explicitly mentioned that investment is not very sensitive to fluctuations in the interest rate, and that investment depends crucially on the entrepreneur's subjective expectation of the future profitability of investment projects.

The first group of 'neoclassical' investment models has been much contributed to by Jorgenson and his colleagues. Their main idea was that given the output and technology of firms, one can derive the optimal capital stock, and investment occurs to fill the gap between the optimal capital stock and the inherited capital stock. As there is no explicit mechanism in which the investment rate is determined, these empirical models employ 'ad hoc' adjustment mechanisms such as delivery lags to allow for the dynamic adjustment of the capital stock generally found in the data.

The main drawback of these models is that the investment rate is indeterminate inside the model and only becomes determinate when one introduces 'ad hoc' mechanisms such as distributed lags. Therefore, even if the empirical performance of these investment equations is typically quite good, their theoretical consistency has often been questioned. Lucas (1967), Gould (1968) and Treadway (1969), in a series of studies, introduced 'adjustment costs' into the firm's profit maximization problem and showed that the optimal investment rate could be derived explicitly in these models. From this work the dynamic neoclassical models have emerged.

This second group is represented mainly by the Q model of investment. Although this model was suggested by Tobin (1969),[1] it was later found that the Q model can be derived from the neoclassical adjustment costs theory (see Hayashi 1982). The Q model can incorporate forward-looking expectations into the Q ratio and is theoretically consistent in that it is obtained from the adjustment costs model. Nevertheless, the empirical performance of this model has not proved to be as successful as the theoretical side.

Given this background, we will now review the investment models to be used in Chapter 6. The main models covered will be the accelerator model, the error correction model introduced by Bean (1981), the Q model and the Euler equation model.

Accelerator-type models

A sales-accelerator model Let us consider a firm and assume it has a putty-putty technology and perfect foresight. We also assume there are no adjustment costs, taxes or debt finance.

The present discounted value of the firm V_t will be written as

$$V_t = \sum_{j=0}^{\infty} \beta_{t+j}\left[P_{t+j}F(K_{t+j},L_{t+j}) - w_{t+j}L_{t+j} - P^I_{t+j}I_{t+j}\right] \qquad (5.1)$$

where β is the discount rate, K is the capital stock, L is the labour input, F(K,L) is the production function, P is the price of output, w is the wage, P^I is the price of investment goods and I is gross investment.

If we maximize V_t subject to $K_{t+j} = (1-\delta)\, K_{t+j-1} + I_{t+j}$, where δ is the rate of depreciation, from the first order condition we find the relation

$$\left(\frac{\partial F}{\partial K}\right)_t = \frac{P^I_t}{P_t}\left(1 - \frac{1-\delta}{1+r_{t+1}} \cdot \frac{P^I_{t+1}}{P^I_t}\right) = J_t \tag{5.2}$$

$$\approx \frac{P^I_t}{P_t}\left(r_{t+1} + \delta - \pi^I_{t+1}\right).$$

In equation (5.2), J_t is the user cost of capital, r_{t+1} is the nominal required rate of return, δ is the depreciation rate and π^I is the inflation rate in terms of investment goods prices. Therefore, equation (5.2) shows that at the optimum capital stock the marginal product of capital equals the cost of using an additional unit of capital.

If F is a constant returns to scale Cobb-Douglas production function, that is if output $Y_t = F(K_t,L_t) = A\, K_t^{\alpha} L_t^{1-\alpha}$, then

$$\left(\frac{\partial F}{\partial K_t}\right) = \alpha\, A\, K_t^{\alpha-1} L^{1-\alpha} = \alpha\left(\frac{Y_t}{K_t}\right) = J_t \tag{5.3}$$

$$\text{or } K^*_t = \alpha\left(\frac{Y_t}{J_t}\right)$$

at the optimum level of the capital stock K^*_t.

If we further assume either that the cost of capital, J_t, is constant or that there is no substitution between capital and other factors, equation (5.3) reduces to

$$K^*_t = \alpha\, Y_t. \tag{5.4}$$

The assumption of a fixed capital-output ratio is a key component of accelerator-type models of investment.

If we now substitute in for K_t from the equation of motion, $K_t = (1-\delta)K_{t-1} + I_t$, we obtain

$$I_t = \alpha Y_t - (1 - \delta)K_{t-1}. \tag{5.5}$$

If we divide both sides of equation (5.5) by K_{t-1}, we get the basis of our accelerator-type investment model used in Chapter 6 as

$$\left(\frac{I_t}{K_{t-1}}\right) = \alpha \left(\frac{Y_t}{K_{t-1}}\right) + \text{constant}. \tag{5.6}$$

Equation (5.6) can be interpreted as a steady-state or long-run relationship. We can embed this long-run relationship into a dynamic regression model, to reflect the fact that the capital stock may not adjust immediately to changes in output. This gives a dynamic model of the form

$$\left(\frac{I_t}{K_{t-1}}\right) = \rho \left(\frac{I_{t-1}}{K_{t-2}}\right) + \beta_0\left(\frac{Y_t}{K_{t-1}}\right) + \beta_1\left(\frac{Y_{t-1}}{K_{t-2}}\right) + \text{constant} \tag{5.7}$$

where $\left(\frac{\beta_0 + \beta_1}{1 - \rho}\right) = \alpha$. This type of model was used in the study of financial constraints and investment by Fazzari, Hubbard and Petersen (1988).

Accelerator-type investment models have been criticised for a number of reasons.

First, the model does not explicitly consider the adjustment of the actual capital stock to its optimum level, and the dynamic structure of the regression models is completely 'ad hoc'. Without the imposition of some external adjustment mechanism, the investment rate becomes indeterminate. The assumption of putty-putty technology may also be unrealistic.

Second, as Y_t depends on K_t and K_t depends on I_t, it is likely that Y_t is correlated with shocks to current investment, and therefore simultaneity bias occurs. This can of course be avoided by using instrumental variable estimation methods, but this is frequently ignored.

Third, there is no explicit role in these models for expectations of future profitability. As we discuss below, this also arises as a result of neglecting the process of dynamic adjustment. One consequence is that current financial variables that help to forecast future profitability may appear to be significant in these models, even in the absence of any financial constraints on investment.

An error correction model Bean (1981) suggested another non-structural investment model that incorporates the firm's long-run optimal capital stock into the short-run investment model by introducing an 'error correction' term. This model was an innovation in the sense that it characterised a rational response by economic agents under uncertainty more clearly than in the Jorgenson-type accelerator models. However, the model is criticised for the same reasons as the basic accelerator model, in that investment is depicted as a backward-looking process.

From the first order condition as in equation (5.2), we can obtain the optimal capital stock assuming a constant returns to scale and constant elasticity of substitution production function, giving

$$K_t^* = A\, Y_t\, J_t^{-\sigma} \tag{5.8}$$

where σ is the elasticity of substitution between capital and labour. The Cobb-Douglas case emerges when $\sigma=1$ (see equation (5.3)), and the simple accelerator model when $\sigma=0$ (see equation (5.4)).

Now taking logs of both sides of equation (5.8) gives

$$k_t^* = a + y_t - \sigma j_t \tag{5.9}$$

where the lower case letters denote natural logarithms. If we regard equation (5.9) as the long-run desired relation in the steady state, this can be included as the error correction mechanism in the context of an error correction model. This takes the form

$$\Delta k_t = \alpha + \beta(L)\Delta k_{t-1} + \gamma(L)\Delta y_t + \delta(L)\Delta j_t - \phi[k_{t-p} - a - y_{t-p} + \sigma j_{t-p}] + \varepsilon_t \qquad (5.10)$$

where $\beta(L)$, $\gamma(L)$ and $\delta(L)$ are polynomials in the lag operator L, and ε_t is an error term.

The error correction term on the right hand side can be simplified to $-\phi[k_{t-p} - y_{t-p}] - \psi j_{t-p}$ + constant. The dependent variable Δk_t can also be transformed as follows

$$\Delta k_t \approx \frac{K_t - K_{t-1}}{K_{t-1}} = \frac{K_t}{K_{t-1}} - 1. \qquad (5.11)$$

From the relation $K_t = (1-\delta)K_{t-1} + I_t$, we substitute in for K_t in equation (5.11) to obtain

$$\Delta k_t \approx \frac{(1-\delta)K_{t-1} + I_t}{K_{t-1}} - 1 = \frac{I_t}{K_{t-1}} - \delta. \qquad (5.12)$$

If we incorporate these adjustments into equation (5.10), we get[2]

$$\frac{I_t}{K_{t-1}} = \alpha + \beta(L)\frac{I_{t-1}}{K_{t-2}} + \gamma(L)\Delta y_t + \delta(L)\Delta j_t - \phi[k_{t-p} - y_{t-p}] - \psi j_{t-p} + \varepsilon_t. \qquad (5.13)$$

In principle this model allows for more flexible substitution between capital and labour than the basic sales-accelerator model. We will consider this model in our empirical analysis in Chapter 6, although it shares with the sales-accelerator model the features of a backward-looking model with an 'ad hod' dynamic structure.

Adjustment cost models

Unlike the traditional models we dealt with in the previous section, the main feature of more recent investment models is that they explicitly incorporate costs of adjusting the capital stock and therefore they characterise the adjustment path for the capital stock when it is away from the static optimum level. This also results in a more explicit treatment of forward-looking expectations.

Consider a firm whose objective is to maximise the net present value V_t in period t, again in the absence of debt and taxes,

$$V_t = E_t\Big[\sum_{j=0}^{\infty} \beta_{t+j}\Pi_{t+j}\Big] \tag{5.14}$$

where $E_t[.]$ denotes the conditional expectation based on information available in period t, Π_{t+j} is the net cash flow in period t+j and β_{t+j} is the discount factor between period t and period t+j, given by

$$\beta_{t+j} = \prod_{i=1}^{j} (1+r_{t+i})^{-1} \quad j=1,2, \ldots ,\infty, \quad \beta_t = 1 \tag{5.15}$$

where r_{t+1} is the required nominal rate of return between period t and t+1, which is assumed to be given exogenously to the firm.

The net cash flow is now given by

$$\Pi_t = \Pi(K_t,L_t,I_t) = P_t[F(K_t,L_t) - G(I_t,K_t)] - w_tL_t - P^I_tI_t \tag{5.16}$$

where G(.) is the adjustment cost function and all other notation was defined in early this section. These costs of adjustment are assumed to be strictly convex in investment and take the form of lost output. In this model, capital goods are assumed to be homogeneous, and the only quasi-fixed factor of production.

Suppose that the firm maximises net present value in equation (5.14) subject to the capital accumulation constraint

$$K_t = (1-\delta)\, K_{t-1} + I_t \tag{5.17}$$

where δ is the rate of depreciation as before. Substituting in this constraint for K_t, the firm's objective function can be written in the dynamic programming form

$$V_t(K_{t-1}) = \Pi((1-\delta)K_{t-1} + I_t, L_t, I_t) + E_t\left[\beta_{t+1} V_{t+1}((1-\delta)K_{t-1} + I_t)\right] \tag{5.18}$$

Differentiating this expression with respect to I_t, K_{t-1} and L_t gives the first-order conditions

$$0 = (\partial\Pi/\partial K)_t + (\partial\Pi/\partial I)_t + E_t\left[\beta_{t+1} V'_{t+1}\right] \tag{5.19}$$

$$V'_t = (1-\delta)(\partial\Pi/\partial K)_t + (1-\delta)E_t\left[\beta_{t+1} V'_{t+1}\right] \tag{5.20}$$

$$0 = (\partial\Pi/\partial L)_t \tag{5.21}$$

where $V'_t = (\partial V_t/\partial K_{t-1})$ is the shadow value of an additional unit of capital. The second condition is the Euler equation which describes the evolution of this shadow value along the optimal adjustment path, and the third condition is the standard marginal productivity condition for optimal variable inputs.

From equation (5.19) and (5.20), we can derive a more intuitive first-order condition as

$$V'_t = -\,(1-\delta)(\partial\Pi/\partial I)_t. \tag{5.22}$$

Equation (5.22) shows that the increase in the value of the firm from having one additional unit of capital at t-1 (which implies (1-δ) additional units of capital at t) is equal to cost of acquiring (1-δ)

units of capital at t; that is, the marginal benefit is equal to the marginal cost of additional units of capital.

Although equations (5.20) and (5.22) exactly describe how investment occurs in this framework, they are not yet an empirical investment model since the shadow value V_t' is not observable. The Q model and the Euler equation model which will be described below employ different methods to make these conditions estimable. The Q model imposes auxiliary assumptions that allow the unobservable shadow value of capital to be related to the observable ratio between the stock market's valuation of the firm and its capital stock at replacement cost. That is, the observed market valuation of firms is used to 'measure' V_t'. In contrast, the Euler equation approach utilises both equations to eliminate V_t' so that equation (5.20) can be written in terms of observables. The Euler equation is, in essence, an intertemporal condition relating current investment to last period's investment and marginal product of capital, which can be estimated directly.

The Q model of investment If we first assume that the firm faces the perfect competition in all markets, we can write

$$(\partial\Pi/\partial I)_t = - P_t(\partial G/\partial I)_t - P_t^I \tag{5.23}$$

$$(\partial\Pi/\partial K)_t = P_t[(\partial F/\partial K)_t - (\partial G/\partial K)_t]. \tag{5.24}$$

Using equation (5.23) in (5.22) gives

$$\left(\frac{\partial G}{\partial I}\right)_t = \left(\frac{\lambda_t}{P_t^I} - 1\right)\frac{P_t^I}{P_t} = (q_t - 1)\frac{P_t^I}{P_t} \tag{5.25}$$

where $\lambda_t = (\partial V_t/\partial K_{t-1})/(1-\delta)$ and $q_t = \lambda_t/P_t^I$ are the shadow value of one extra unit of capital in period t and marginal Q respectively. Here, the marginal Q measures the ratio of the shadow value λ_t to the price of one extra unit of uninstalled capital. This is the foundation of the Q model. In equation (5.25), we observe that all expectations about the firm's future costs, revenues and profitability relevant for the investment decision are summarised in the shadow value λ_t and therefore in marginal q.

However, to use equation (5.25) as an empirical investment model, it is still necessary that we specify a functional form for the adjustment cost function and replace the unobservable shadow value by some observable counterpart.

First, Summers (1981) has suggested a convenient form for the adjustment cost function, namely,

$$G(I_t,K_t) = \frac{b}{2}\left[\left(\frac{I}{K}\right)_t - c\right]^2 K_t \tag{5.26}$$

which is strictly convex in I_t and homogeneous of degree one in (I_t,K_t). G(.) is a quadratic function of the investment rate $(I/K)_t$ and marginal adjustment costs are therefore linear in the observed rate of investment.

In this case, equation (5.25) can be written as

$$\left(\frac{I}{K}\right)_t = c + \frac{1}{b}\left[(q_t-1)\frac{P^I_t}{P_t}\right]. \tag{5.27}$$

In the above equation q_t is still the unobservable marginal q. To measure marginal Q we require the additional assumption that both the production function $F(K_t,L_t)$ and the adjustment cost function $G(I_t,K_t)$ are homogeneous of degree one in their arguments. We also need the assumption that the stock market is strongly efficient so that we can measure V_t as the stock market valuation of the company. Under these conditions, Hayashi (1982) showed that marginal Q is simply related to the observable average Q ratio, transforming equation (5.27) as follows

$$\left(\frac{I}{K}\right)_t = c + \frac{1}{b}\left[\frac{V_t}{(1-\delta)P^I_t K_{t-1}} - 1\right]\frac{P^I_t}{P_t} = c + \frac{1}{b}Q_t \qquad (5.28)$$

where $V_t/(1-\delta)P^I_t K_{t-1}$ is the average Q ratio, whose relation to investment was first discussed by Keynes (1936) and Tobin (1969).

If the definition of V_t is extended to include the debt of the firm and to introduce corporate income tax (provided either that taxable income is never negative, or that tax losses are treated in a symmetric way to taxable profits), then the tax-adjusted Q is (see Hayashi 1982)

$$Q_t = \left[\frac{V_t + B_t - A_t}{(1-\delta)P^I_t(1-\eta_t)K_{t-1}} - 1\right]\frac{P^I_t(1-\eta_t)}{P_t(1-\tau_t)} \qquad (5.29)$$

where V_t is the stock market valuation of the firm, B_t is the market value of the firm's debt and other net liabilities, τ_t is the statutory corporate tax rate, η_t is the present value of current and future depreciation allowances associated with an additional unit of investment in period t, and A_t is the present value of all current and future depreciation allowances that the firm can claim in respect of past investments. The basic idea is that the numerator of average Q measures the market valuation of the firm's fixed capital, whilst the denominator measures its replacement cost value in the presence of tax. In Chapter 6 we will use a version of equation (5.28) incorporating these tax adjustments.

The contribution and features of the Q model can be summarised as follows.

First, as the Q ratio involves the stock market valuation of the firm's capital, it explicitly incorporates expectations about the future profitability of the firm. In the presence of adjustment costs, the lags that are typically included in accelerator-type models will reflect influences on these expectations, as well as the adjustment process. In contrast, all the relevant expectational information is captured in the Q ratio and the Q model is not subjected to the Lucas critique.

Second, the Q model is essentially deterministic. When estimating the model, it is common practice to introduce stochastic variation into the intercept, giving

$$\left(\frac{I}{K}\right)_t = c + \frac{1}{b} Q_t + e_t \tag{5.30}$$

where e_t is interpreted as a shock to marginal adjustment costs. But it is important to note that there is no obvious reason to believe that this technology shock must follow an innovation process.

Third, in equation (5.30), the current Q_t is inevitably correlated with the current shock e_t. It is clear from equation (5.20) that λ_t and therefore V_t is affected by the current shock to adjustment costs, even if this disturbance happens to be an innovation. This endogeneity should be taken into account when considering suitable estimators for the model. In particular, one should avoid estimators which require strict exogeneity in applications using panel data.

An Euler equation model Perhaps the main drawback of the Q model is that to obtain an observable measure of the shadow value of capital, we require strong auxiliary assumptions that are not themselves implied by the underlying theory of optimal investment subject to adjustment costs. Abel (1980) developed the Euler equation approach in the investment literature, based on the optimal relationship between marginal adjustment costs in adjacent periods, and not requiring a measure of the shadow value.

Provided that equation (5.22) holds not only for period t but can also be expected to hold for period t+1, we have

$$\lambda_t - (1-\delta)E_t[\beta_{t+1}\lambda_{t+1}] = -(\partial\Pi/\partial I)_t + (1-\delta)E_t[\beta_{t+1}(\partial\Pi/\partial I)_{t+1}]. \tag{5.31}$$

We can use this relation to eliminate the unobservable shadow value λ_t from the Euler equation (5.20), giving

$$-(1-\delta)E_t[\beta_{t+1}(\partial\Pi/\partial I)_{t+1}] = -(\partial\Pi/\partial I)_t - (\partial\Pi/\partial K)_t. \tag{5.32}$$

Notice that in this expression the one step ahead forecast of marginal adjustment costs controls for all relevant expectations. Denoting the forecast error made in period t for $\beta_{t+1}(\partial\Pi/\partial I)_{t+1}$ by $\varepsilon_{t+1} = \beta_{t+1}(\partial\Pi/\partial I)_{t+1} - E_t[\beta_{t+1}(\partial\Pi/\partial I)_{t+1}]$, substituting the realised value for the one-period ahead expectation then gives

$$-(1-\delta)\beta_{t+1}(\partial\Pi/\partial I)_{t+1} = -(\partial\Pi/\partial I)_t - (\partial\Pi/\partial K)_t + (1-\delta)\varepsilon_{t+1}. \tag{5.33}$$

To derive an empirical investment model, we only need to specify marginal adjustment costs and the marginal revenue product of capital in terms of observables.

Following Bond and Meghir (1994a), the firm's net revenue function and the adjustment cost function are assumed to take the same form as in the Q model, in which case marginal adjustment costs are again linear in the investment rate, and for a price-taking firm this gives

$$(\partial\Pi/\partial I)_t = -bP_t\left(\frac{I}{K}\right)_t + bcP_t - P^I_t. \tag{5.34}$$

To obtain an expression for the marginal revenue product of capital, we rely on the linear homogeneity of F(.) and G(.). From these assumptions, the Euler equation can be rearranged to give an empirical investment model as

$$\left(\frac{I}{K}\right)_{t+1} = c(1-\phi_{t+1}) + (1+c)\phi_{t+1}\left(\frac{I}{K}\right)_t - \phi_{t+1}\left(\frac{I}{K}\right)^2_t - \frac{\phi_{t+1}}{b}\left(\frac{\Pi^o}{K}\right)_t + \frac{\phi_{t+1}}{b}J_t + v_{t+1} \tag{5.35}$$

where $\phi_{t+1} = \frac{1+\rho_{t+1}}{1-\delta}$, ρ_{t+1} is the real discount rate defined by $1+\rho_{t+1} = \frac{p_t}{p_{t+1}}(1+r_{t+1})$, $(\Pi^o/K)_t = \left(\frac{P_tY_t - w_tL_t}{P_tK_t}\right)$ is the ratio of real gross operating profit to the capital stock, and J_t is the Jorgenson user cost of capital as defined in equation (5.2).

According to the theory, the coefficient on the lagged dependent variable is expected to be greater than one while the coefficient on the squared investment term is expected to be expected to be less than minus one. The coefficient on the lagged gross operating profit term is expected to be negative and depends on the magnitude of adjustment costs. Note that this profit term appears in the model to measure the marginal profitability of capital under the assumption of constant returns to scale, and not as a result of capital market imperfections.

If we introduce monopolistic competition into this model, one additional term in the ratio of output to capital is introduced into the basic specification (see Bond and Meghir 1994a). The coefficient on this extra term is expected to be positive, although a positive coefficient on this term could also indicate non-constant returns to scale. In Chapter 6 we will use a version of equation (5.35) which allows for monopolistic competition.

5.3 Financial factors and investment

The Modigliani-Miller theorem and subsequent developments

As far as the impact of financial factors on investment decisions is concerned, there has been a discontinuity in the literature. In the 1950s, Meyer and Kuh (1957) emphasized the importance of financial considerations in investment decisions, using firm-level data. However, since Modigliani and Miller (1958) provided a theoretical basis for the argument that real investment decisions are separable from the financial structure of firms, this Modigliani-Miller theorem has until recently dominated both the theoretical and empirical study of company investment. Their core argument was that a firm's financial structure will not affect its market value in perfect capital markets. Thus, in a perfect capital market setting, with no taxes or transaction costs and with symmetric information, the cost of internal funds and external funds is exactly the same, and therefore the real investment decision is not affected by whether it is financed from retained earnings, or debt or new equity. Much of the development of investment theories and empirical research on investment has assumed the Modigliani-Miller theorem. Moreover, econometric evidence from studies of aggregate investment data did not appear to reject the view that financial structure is irrelevant for real investment decisions.

However, the last decade has seen a gradual erosion in the influence of the Modigliani-Miller theorem. This view has been challenged by both theoretical and empirical studies. Two important developments have happened in the literature. First, a group of theoretical contributions have shown how the costs of internal and external finance may differ in the context of imperfect capital markets (see Myers and Majluf 1984, Greenwald, Stiglitz and Weiss 1984). The 'hierarchy of finance' or 'pecking order' model assumes that internally generated finance for investment is available at lower cost than external finance. Although the potential reasons for this phenomenon are numerous, among the most prominent are transaction costs, tax advantages, agency problems, costs of financial distress, and asymmetric information. In the US, for example, there are differences in the tax treatment of dividend income and capital gains. For most taxpayers dividend income is taxed more heavily than capital gains, so that shareholders pay less tax when dividend payments are minimized. This makes retained earnings the tax-efficient source of investment finance. Other countries, however, do not always have the same tax structure, so that the tax preference for internal finance can be reversed.

In Korea, while the system of corporate taxation is very similar to that in the the US,[3] there are some important differences in the treatment of personal taxation. Most importantly, dividend income is taxed even more heavily in Korea; although there is no personal taxation of capital gains, dividend income is taxed at marginal rates as high as 70 % for wealthy investors (see Kim 1990). Thus, there exists a significant tax advantage of minimising the level of dividends, giving a tax preference for internal finance. However, Dailami (1990) observed that the dividend pay-out ratio in the Korean corporate sector averaged 28 % over the period 1975-1986, mainly because it was mandatory by law until the late 1960s that companies maintained a defined minimum amount of dividend payments, irrespective of the tax consequences for shareholders.

A more general reason for this hierarchy of costs may be asymmetric information between firms and suppliers of external finance. For example, if the manager has access to better information about investment projects, the lender tends to charge a 'lemons' premium which reflects this informational disadvantage. At any rate, this new theoretical development has been incorporated into investment models.

The second important development is that the availability of panel data on companies has made it possible for empirical studies to move beyond the assumption of a representative firm. When one estimates investment functions using aggregate data, it is assumed that all firms are homogeneous so that when, for example, aggregate investment is not found to be highly sensitive to financial variables, it may be that a strong sensitivity for some firms is dominated in the aggregate by the insensitivity of the remainder of the sample. With panel data, it has now become possible to explicitly consider firm heterogeneity in the estimation of investment models.

Among other considerations, these two important developments have contributed to our understanding of the relationship between financial factors and corporate investment. The main questions in the empirical analysis of investment and financial constraints using company accounts data were first whether corporate investment is sensitive to financial factors, and secondly, whether this sensitivity differs according to the characteristics of different types of firms.

Hierarchy of finance model: the concepts

As was discussed above, the hierarchy of finance model starts from the assumption or observation that external finance from debt and new share issues can be more expensive than internal finance from retained earnings.

To illustrate the effect of this financing hierarchy on investment, we can consider a firm whose financing costs are subject to the hierarchy discussed above.[4] In Figure 5.1(a), we first focus on the case in which the firm uses only retained earnings or new equity. The required rate of return r_R shows the cost of finance from retained earnings, while the higher rate of return r_N shows the cost of finance from new share issues. The level of investment spending $\bar{I}$ shows the maximum level of investment spending that the firm can finance from its internal sources.[5] The downward sloping curves D_1, D_2, and D_3 depict three possible investment opportunity sets available to the firm. When the firm's investment opportunity curve is D_1, the firm can finance all its desired investment I_1 (which is below $\bar{I}$) from retained profits and still pay out a relatively high dividend. When the level of available internal finance increases to $\bar{I}'$, the investment level (I_1) is not affected at all. When the demand curve is D_3 and marginal investment is financed by issuing new shares, the investment level (I_3) is also not affected by fluctuations in the supply of internal finance. But when the firm's demand for investment is like D_2, the level of investment is constrained by the availability of low-cost internal finance, and in this case fluctuations in internal finance (cash flow) directly affect the level of investment (i.e. which increases from $\bar{I}$ to $\bar{I}'$).

Figure 5.1(b) describes the case where debt finance is also used. In this case, the firm can finance higher investment above $\bar{I}$ by borrowing, to the extent that it finds it worthwhile to bear the increasing cost. As before, a windfall increase in cash flow does not affect the investment level when the demand curve is like D_1 or D_3. But when the demand curve is like D_2, the fluctuation in cash flow again influences the level of investment (i.e. which increases from I_2 to I_2'). To sum up, the implication is that there may be some firms whose investment is affected by financial constraints, in that even a windfall increase in cash flow (which has no effect on the position of the investment demand curve) results in higher investment.

The role of financial variables in econometric investment equations

In the framework of the hierarchy of finance model, we observed that the investment of some firms may be affected by financial constraints in the sense that if desired investment spending is greater than the supply of internal finance then it can be influenced by windfall changes in cash flow. It is sometimes suggested in the literature that this impact of financial constraints can be tested by including additional financial variables like cash flow in econometric investment equations. The coefficients on these financial variables are suggested as a measure of the sensitivity of investment to financial constraints.

However it is crucial to point out that such econometric results should be interpreted with more qualification. In accelerator-type models, as we have seen in section 5.2, the investment decision was essentially modelled by some backward-looking function of observed variables, such as

$$I_t = f(Y_t, Y_{t-1}, J_t, J_{t-1}, K_{t-1}). \tag{5.36}$$

In adjustment cost models, we saw that investment will also depend on expected future output and costs, as reflected for example in the Q variable. However, in empirical accelerator models, these expectations are implicitly assumed to be simply related to the current and past observed values of output and the user cost. The problem is that accelerator-type models do not distinguish between the factors which directly influence the optimal level of the capital stock and other variables which simply help to forecast the future values of such factors (see Bond and Meghir 1994b).

Current profit or cash flow variables may therefore appear to be significant in such econometric models, even for firms that are not affected by financial constraints. For example, an increase in profitability that is perceived to be persistent will shift outwards the investment demand curve in Figure 5.1, and will result in higher investment for this reason alone. For this reason, the significance of cash flow terms in accelerator-type models does not guarantee that investment is affected by financial constraints.

There are two basic responses to this problem in the empirical literature which investigates financial constraints on investment.
First, structural models like the Q and Euler equation models have tended to replace accelerator-type models in testing the sensitivity of investment to financial constraints. In the Q model, as we saw in the second part of section 5.2, it can be shown that under certain conditions the Q variable summarises all expectations that are relevant for investment behaviour. Unlike in an accelerator model, the effect of cash flow on expectations of future demand or costs of capital is already captured by the measured Q ratio. Blundell, Bond, Devereux and Schiantarelli (1992) and Hayashi and Inoue (1991) both used the Q model to test the sensitivity of investment to cash flow. Bond and Meghir (1994a) and Whited (1992) used the Euler equation model to investigate this issue. We review this literature further in section 5.4 below.

Second, efforts have also been made to examine the different effect of cash flow on investment across sub-samples of firms that may be believed *a priori* to be affected differently by financial constraints. Fazzari, Hubbard and Petersen (1988) divided their sample of US firms into three classes according to dividend pay-out behaviour. Devereux and Schiantarelli (1990) divided their sample of UK firms according to firm size, age, and type of industry.

In this section we consider some predictions of the hierarchy of finance approach for the impact of financial constraints on different types of firms in Korea.

In Chapter 2 we argued that the enduring effects of government financial intervention has favoured firms with certain characteristics, thus leaving a segmented market for investment finance. In Chapter 4 we saw that different types of Korean firms have indeed relied on different sources of investment finance during the 1980s. We can now apply the hierarchy of finance approach to consider the impact of government intervention in Korea and to test the hypothesis that certain types of Korean manufacturing firms have enjoyed a relatively low cost of external finance. We examine various cases in which one type of firm is more affected by financial constraints on investment than another type of firm. We suppose that Type 1 firms face either a lower cost of new equity or a less steeply increasing cost of debt than Type 2 firms.

In Figure 5.2(a), we first abstract from debt finance and suppose that Type 2 firms face a much higher cost of issuing new shares (C_2) than do Type 1 firms (C_1). Both firms face the same cost of internal finance and the same investment demand curve D. At the level of internal finance indicated by $\bar{I}$, we observe that the level of investment for Type 2 firms is constrained at the level $\bar{I}$, whilst the level of investment for Type 1 firms will be I_1.

Now consider a windfall increase in the availability of internal finance, by the same amount for both types of firms, from $\bar{I}$ to $\bar{I}'$. In this case, there is an increase in the investment of Type 2 firms from $\bar{I}$ to $\bar{I}'$, but no change in the investment of Type 1 firms.

This example illustrates the key prediction that firms who enjoy a privileged access to external finance are less likely to be affected by financial constraints on investment than firms who are not so favoured by government intervention in the financial system.

In Figure 5.2(b), we introduce debt finance. Here Type 2 firms face a more steeply increasing cost of debt than Type 1 firms. This could arise from a direct government subsidy to borrowing by Type 1 firms, or from a government commitment to assist Type 1 firms in the event of financial distress. When there is a windfall increase in cash flow, the investment of Type 2 firms increases by the relatively large amount $I_2' - I_2$, whilst the investment of Type 1 firms increases by the much smaller amount $I_1' - I_1$. We come to the same conclusion from these two examples, that when there are two types of firms whose cost of external finance are different, the investment of the type whose cost is higher is more likely to be significantly affected by financial constraints than the investment of the type whose cost is lower, provided that their investment opportunities and the availability of internal finance are reasonably similar.

We will use this framework to motivate our empirical analysis in Chapter 6. In the Korean context, we consider affiliation to Chaebol groups and firm size to be prominent factors that may well have made the cost of external finance significantly lower for group-affiliated firms and for large firms. In Chapter 2 we discussed how this capital market 'imperfection' may have been the deliberate intention of government intervention in the financial system, although even in the absence of government interference such firms could enjoy important advantages in financial markets characterised by imperfect information.

In our analysis of the sources of finance for company investment in Chapter 4, we observed that group-affiliated firms and large firms had used a lower share of finance from internal sources (and a higher share of long-term loans) than non-group-affiliated firms and smaller firms. This pattern may also be consistent with a relatively high cost of external finance facing non-group or small firms. This pattern is illustrated in Figure 5.3 under the assumption that the two types of firms face the same position of the investment demand curve and have the same supply of internal finance. The share of debt finance for non-group firms $((I_{NG}-\bar{I})/I_{NG})$ is relatively low in this situation, whilst the share of internal finance for non-group firms $(\bar{I}/I_{NG})$ is relatively high.

It is of course also possible that this financing pattern has arisen for different reasons, perhaps because non-group firms and small firms faced a weaker demand for investment compared to group firms and large firms, or because their supply of internal finance was relatively high. We believe that the question of whether investment is affected by financial constraints more significantly for certain types of firms than for other types of firms is better investigated through a rigorous microeconometric analysis using company panel data. This question will form a major part of our investigation for Korean companies in Chapter 6. In the last section of this chapter, we review some of the existing econometric evidence.

5.4 Survey of previous econometric results

In the last decade, there has been a growing interest in the use of firm-level panel data obtained from company accounts to estimate empirical investment models. Some studies in this vein have focused mainly on evaluating the performance of the Q model at the level of firm, given the widespread recognition that the empirical results when using aggregate data were rather disappointing, and that these poor results may reflect aggregation bias rather than theoretical mis-specification. Examples of this group include Blundell, Bond, Devereux and Schiantarelli (1992), Hayashi and Inoue (1991) and Schaller (1990).

These studies are complemented by a group of papers that investigate the relationship between financial factors and investment spending in a more direct way. Important studies include Fazzari, Hubbard and Petersen (1988), Hoshi, Kashyap and Scharfstein (1991), Devereux and Schiantarelli (1990), Whited (1992) and Bond and Meghir (1994a).

There are several common themes in these studies. First, by estimating a Q model or an Euler equation model, they aim to investigate how financial factors influence investment spending whilst controlling for the effect of financial variables on expectations of future profitability. While the first group of papers used total samples to test for the effect of cash flow on investment, the second group divided firms into sub-samples on the basis of certain sample separation criteria and offered more direct tests of the hierarchy of finance model.

Second, most (but not all) of these studies have used appropriate estimators, taking into account the endogeneity of the explanatory variables. The Q model theoretically implies a correlation between current Q and shocks to the investment equation. Most of the above studies have recognised this and used instrumental variable methods, particularly generalised method of moments (GMM) estimators. Most of them have also controlled for the influence of unobserved firm-specific effects.

Applications of the Q model

Blundell, Bond, Devereux and Schiantarelli (1992) estimate a Q model on disaggregated panel data for 532 UK manufacturing firms over the period 1975 to 1986. They experiment with various stochastic properties and dynamic structures of the model, which affect the valid instruments for consistent estimation of the parameters. They reject the static specification of the Q model in favour of a dynamic specification, due to the finding of significant autocorrelation in the error term. A dynamic specification which includes both the lagged dependent variable and lagged Q is preferred rejected, with the common factor restriction not being rejected by the data. Based on the theoretical and empirical finding that Q is not only correlated with firm-specific effects but also endogenous with respect to current shocks, their preferred estimator is a differenced GMM estimator which uses only past variables as instruments. Blundell, Bond, Devereux and Schiantarelli (1992) find that the coefficient on tax-adjusted Q is around 0.01, and significantly different from zero.

Blundell, Bond, Devereux and Schiantarelli (1992) also estimate the model using alternative estimators which require stricter assumptions on Q. The estimate from an OLS estimator shows the expected upward bias as firm specific effects are ignored, and that from a Within Groups estimator produces the expected downward bias, due to the short time period covered by the panel.[6]

Finally they also find that both cash flow and output terms are significant when added to the specification. The coefficient on cash flow is positive and significant, in addition to a significant average Q. They argue that the negative coefficient on output may reflect monopolistic product markets, although the hypothesis of parameter stability across time is rejected in this augmented specification.

Hayashi and Inoue (1991) report similar econometric testing of the Q model using a panel of company accounts for 687 Japanese manufacturing firms over the period 1977-1986. The Q model they estimate is different in that the denominator of the Q ratio is constructed using a quantity index of capital inputs, not simply the sum of different nominal capital stocks. This specification results from their theoretical analysis of an investment model with heterogeneous capital goods. They allow the coefficient on Q to take a different value in each year of the sample, and find that this time-variation is statistically significant. In common with Blundell, Bond, Devereux and Schiantarelli (1992), they examine the possible biases due to the fact that Q is endogenous, and prefer first-difference GMM estimators.

The estimate of the coefficient on Q is found to be positive and small, but highly significant for most years of their sample, and for two sub-samples (heavy and light industries). The very small coefficients on Q, ranging from 0.005 to 0.049, imply slow adjustment of the capital stock in response to changes in the shadow value of capital. Although Sargan-Hansen test statistics do not strongly suggest mis-specification, they find that including additional explanatory variables such as cash flow does indicate some mis-specification. The coefficient on cash flow is also highly significant, especially in the early years of the sample period. They also find that in the last three years of their period, when the Japanese financial system was substantially deregulated, the coefficient on cash flow is much more significant for light industries than for heavy industries in their sample, which they argue suggests that light industries may not be competitive, as assumed by the Q theory.

Schaller (1990) studies the investment behaviour of firms using a sample of 188 publicly traded US firms. This paper explores two potential explanations for the poor performance of the empirical Q model: aggregation bias and imperfect competition. He finds that at the aggregate level, higher serial correlation is found than at the firm level, indicating that aggregation is responsible for spurious evidence of dynamic mis-specification. He also finds that when adjustment costs are estimated allowing for heterogeneity among firms, the estimated marginal adjustment cost parameter drops significantly, and thus argues that aggregation is at least partially responsible for an upward bias in estimated adjustment costs.

The above studies aim to examine if, by using firm-level data, the empirical performance of the Q model improves. However the results of these papers are not very different from previous aggregate studies. The addition of cash flow into the model produces highly significant coefficients on this term in most cases. Yet this cannot be construed as a direct test of the hierarchy of finance model, as it may be the case that measured Q only provides a poor proxy for the firm's investment opportunities, and that these cash flow terms simply provide additional information about the expected profitability of investment.

Tests for financial constraints

The second group of papers puts more emphasis on testing the hierarchy of finance model. As we discussed in section 5.3, the hierarchy of finance model assumes that there is a discrepancy between the cost of internal funds and the cost of new equity and debt. The first task of these papers is to divide the sample of firms into groups according to whether their investment is likely to fall in the range that is affected by financial constraints.

Fazzari, Hubbard and Petersen (1988) divide their sample of US manufacturing firms according to whether they are likely to be financially constrained or not, using dividend pay-out behaviour as an indicator. They identify cash-rich firms with those paying high dividends and constrained firms with those paying low or zero dividends. Their results show that the Q variable appears to be more significant and cash flow less significant for the high dividend paying sub-sample, which is in line with the prediction that financial constraints are more important for firms where internal funds are in short supply. However, their results also show that even among the firms that pay high dividends, cash flow remains significant in addition to Q.

Using a similar approach, Hoshi, Kashyap and Scharfstein (1991) divide their sample of Japanese manufacturing companies into two groups on the basis of whether these firms have a close relationship with a main bank through the membership of a Keiretsu industrial group. They argue that the monitoring of such firms by the main bank system reduces the importance of asymmetric information between lenders and borrowers, and that firms which have a link with a main bank are therefore less likely to be affected by financial constraints than firms which do not have such a link. Based on this empirical strategy, they find that measured Q is more significant, and cash flow less significant, for the Keiretsu firms that are closely linked to the main banks.

Bond and Meghir (1994a) investigate similar questions on the relationship between investment and financial constraints using an Euler equation framework similar to equation (5.35).[7] Estimating using an unbalanced sample of 626 UK manufacturing firms in the period 1971 - 1986, they find that the dynamic relationship between the current investment rate and its lagged value is broadly consistent with the optimal path suggested by the adjustments cost model but, at the same time, they find persistent excess sensitivity of investment to a measure of cash flow. To investigate whether the investment of some firms in the sample responds differently to financial constraints than the investment of other firms, they divide this sample according to the firm's financial regime into sub-samples of high dividend and low dividend paying firms, controlling for the endogeneity of this selection. The parameter constancy test across these sub-samples suggests that the sensitivity of investment to cash flow is concentrated in the cases where firms pay low dividends.

Evidence from developing countries

Compared to company accounts data in countries like the US, UK and Japan, the available company accounts data for developing countries typically has fewer observations for each firm, and the accounting items available tend to be less detailed.

However, the company accounts of firms in developing countries presents interesting variation. In most developing countries, the financial market is more segmented than in developed countries, and the asymmetric information problem may be more pronounced in the borrower-lender relationship. It is often the case that the government intervenes directly in the allocation of funds, thus causing the investment and financing behaviour of different types of firms to be heterogeneous in a systematic way.

One feature of the literature using company accounts data for developing countries is that studies are often concerned with testing for parameter differences in investment models estimated for pre-financial reform and post-financial reform sub-periods. But since the data periods available tend to be very short and the data period for sub-samples is often less than 3 years, it is not likely that the comparison of such short sub-periods will produce very robust results. Therefore, our study will concentrate on whether corporate investment was affected by financial constraints over our entire data period.

Harris, Schiantarelli and Siregar (1992) estimate general accelerator-type investment models using a balanced panel of 218 Indonesian firms for the period 1981-1988. The results demonstrate that investment for small firms was more sensitive to cash flow than investment for large firms. After dividing the periods into pre- and post-financial liberalization periods 1981-1984 and 1985-1988, they find that whilst for smaller firms the cash flow term was significant in the early period and its significance did not change very much in the post-liberalization period, for larger firms the cash flow was not significant before the liberalization but became significant after liberalization. From this evidence they suggest that the financial reform was beneficial for smaller firms.

Jaramillo, Schiantarelli and Weiss (1993) use a balanced panel of 420 Ecuadorian firms for the period of 1984-1988. They estimate Euler equation investment models and accelerator-type models for the whole sample and for sub-samples divided by size and age. It is notable that they prefer the Euler equation model to the Q model, the reason being that the former model does not need stock price data given that Ecuador does not have a well developed stock market. They find evidence of a rising supply of funds schedule and financial constraints for small firms and young firms, but not for large firms and old firms. Again they also compare their results between pre-financial reform and post-financial reform periods (using 1986 as the breaking point of the sample), but find no significant differences in the sensitivity of investment to financial variables for each group between these two periods.

The two studies described above both use first-differenced Generalised Method of Moments (GMM) estimators to estimate the investment models.

Kong (1992) estimates a Q model of investment using a balanced panel of 170 Korean manufacturing firms for the period 1982-1989. Using a Within Groups estimator, under the assumption of the strict exogeneity of Q but allowing possible correlation of Q with firm specific effects, he finds that the sensitivity of investment to both Q and cash flow is significant in Korea.[8] After dividing the whole sample into Chaebol group-firms and non-group firms,[9] he finds that investment for non-group firms is more sensitive to cash flow than for group firms for the period 1982-1985. But for the later period, he finds that the ranking of these cash flow effects is reversed. He argues that this reversal may have been caused by the fact that government intervention in the allocation of investment finance was much reduced in the later period, and also that group firms had to finance a higher level of investment in that period.

Atiyas (1992) presented another Korean study using a similar approach to Kong (1992). He estimated a Q model with a balanced panel of 180 Korean manufacturing firms for the period 1984-1988. The model was estimated using a first-differenced GMM estimator to allow for the endogeneity of the explanatory variables. The degree of leverage, output and a stock measure of liquidity were also included as explanatory variables. The results for his total sample showed that investment was sensitive to the measure of liquidity, while the debt variable was not significant. When the total sample was divided into sub-samples according to size and the period was divided into two sub-periods 1984-1986 and 1987-1988, the results showed different patterns for these sub-samples. For smaller firms, the effects of debt and liquidity were significant in the first period but have reduced in the second period. For larger firms, the effects of liquidity and debt were negligible in the early period but became significant in the later period. He argues from this evidence that main effect of financial liberalization seems to have been a redistribution of access to external finance, rather than an overall improvement.

5.5 Conclusion

In this chapter, we reviewed the investment models to be used in Chapter 6, and other issues related to testing whether the investment spending of some types of Korean manufacturing companies is affected by financial constraints. We discussed financial constraints in the context of the hierarchy of finance model, and outlined how this approach can motivate testing for a differential impact of financial variables on investment between Korean firms that are affiliated to Chaebol groups and non-group firms, and also between larger and smaller firms. In the next chapter, we will pursue this approach in an econometric study of Korean company investment.

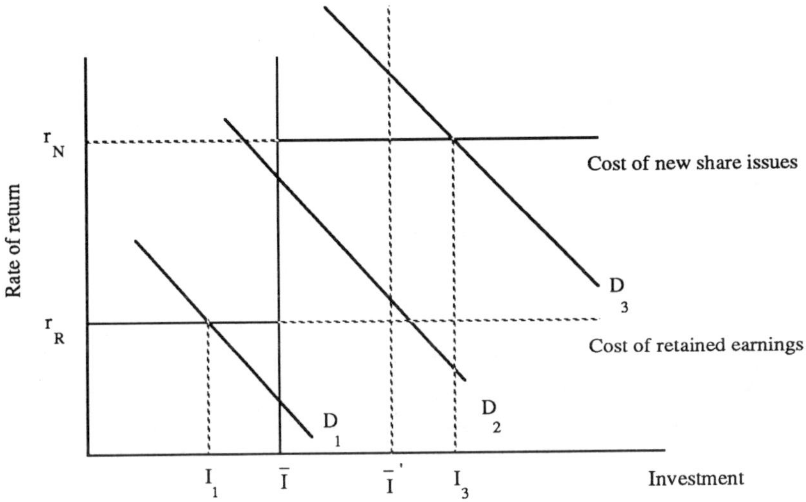

Figure 5.1 (a) The hierarchy of finance model with no debt finance

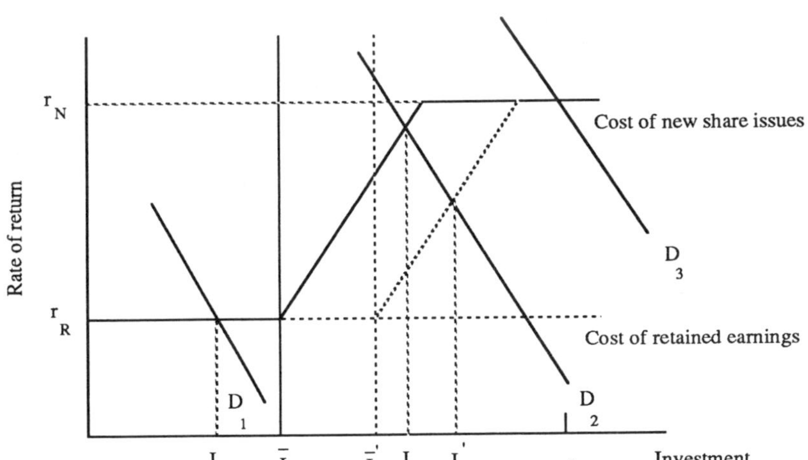

Figure 5.1 (b) The hierarchy of finance model with debt finance

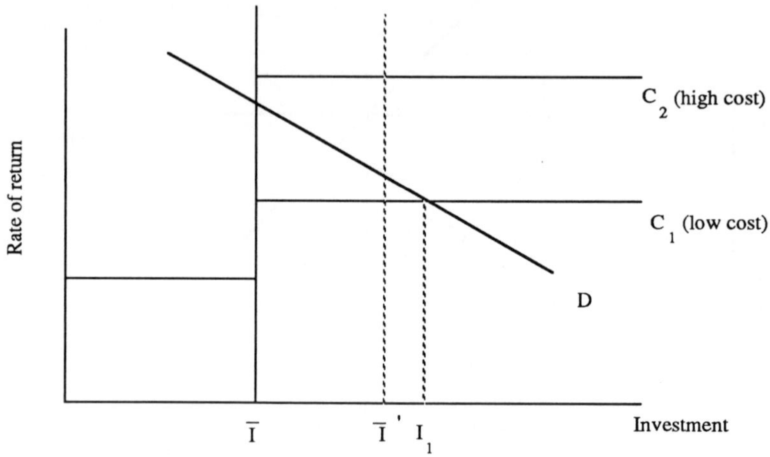

Figure 5.2 (a) Korean case with no debt finance

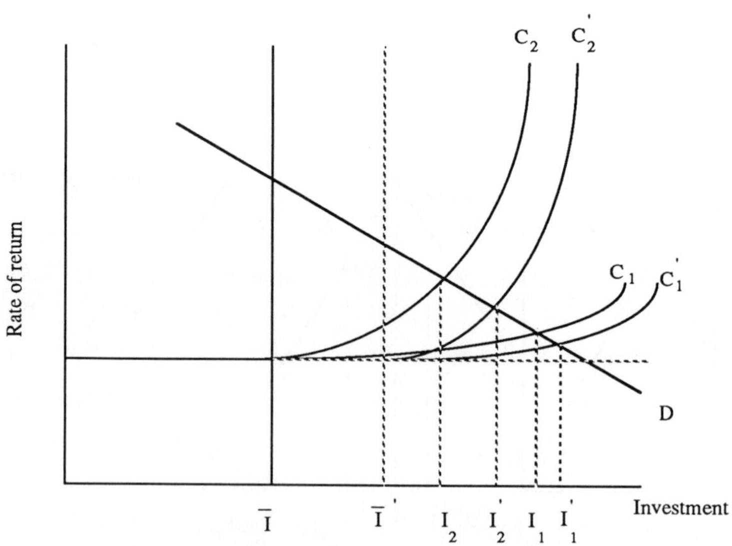

Figure 5.2 (b) Korean case with debt finance

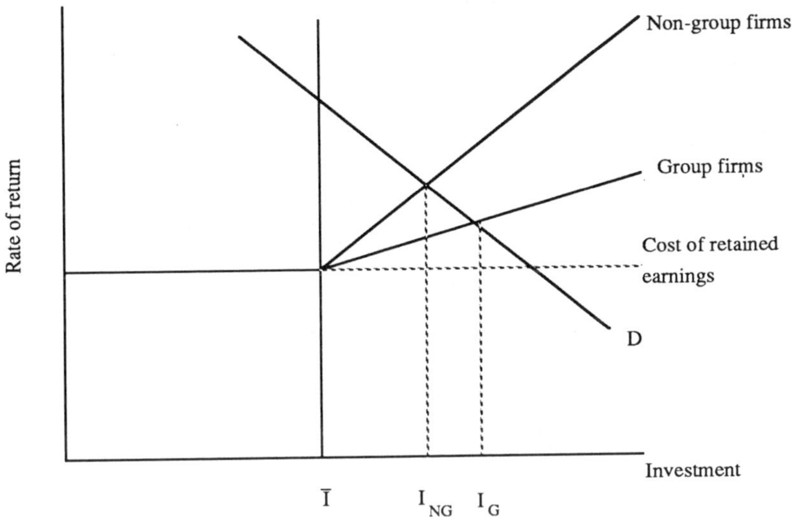

Figure 5.3 Sources of investment finance for group and non-group firms

Notes

1. The basic idea was initially suggested by Keynes (1936), who pointed out the function of the stock market to revalue firms, and the tendency of firms to make investment decisions based on that information.
2. Bean (1981) further transformed the model to avoid using data on the capital stock. We do not follow this step, as we are required to use capital stock data to estimate the other investment models we consider.
3. For example, Korean taxation of dividend income follows the so-called 'classical' system, in that the shareholder's income is taxed both at the company level and again at the personal level.
4. The discussion is adapted from Bond and Meghir (1994b).

5. This level may be associated with zero dividends, but this need not be the case. See Bond and Meghir (1994a) for a model where positive dividends are paid at $\bar{I}$. Legal restrictions on dividend payments in Korea would have a similar effect.
6. The properties of these estimators will be discussed in Chapter 6.
7. See also Whited (1992) and Gilchrist (1991) for other studies using the Euler equation framework.
8. He finds that the sensitivity of investment to cash flow is much higher for companies in Korea than in the US or the UK.
9. Group membership is here defined as belonging to one of the 30 largest Chaebol groups as defined by the Economic Planning Board in Korea.

6 An econometric analysis of company investment and financial constraints using a panel of Korean manufacturing firms

6.1 Introduction

In this chapter, we report a formal econometric analysis of investment behaviour using company accounts data for Korean manufacturing firms. As we argued in Chapter 2, the financial system in Korea is peculiar in that certain types of firms have been consistently favoured, and had access to investment finance at a relatively low cost. The membership of an industrial grouping, called 'Chaebol' in Korea, was one of the principal factors that determined the access of the firm to finance on favoured terms; group-affiliated firms could borrow or issue equity at lower cost than non-group affiliated firms. Firm size, export ratio, age and industry classification have also been suggested as factors that may influence access to privileged finance.

Our empirical strategy in this chapter is to estimate the four investment models that we reviewed in Chapter 5, and to test for the effect of financial variables using both our whole sample and sub-samples divided according to these five sample separation criteria. Cash flow has been used as the main financial variable, and the main focus is on investigating different responses of investment across sub-samples of firms to fluctuations in cash flow.

This chapter proceeds as follows. In the next section, we describe the data and the definition of variables we used for estimation. Further details of this section are presented in the Data Appendix. Various methods of estimating panel data models have been employed in this chapter and these are described in section 6.3. In section 6.4, we present the empirical results for each of our investment models. Finally, in section 6.5, we summarise the main findings and compare our results with similar studies, especially Hoshi, Kashyap and Scharfstein (1991).

6.2 Samples and variables used

Our data are drawn from the published accounts of Korean corporations provided by Korea Investors Service (KIS) Line. As we noted in Chapter 4, our data covers firms that were listed on the stock market by 1991. For the analysis of this chapter, we selected only companies whose main business activity is in the manufacturing sector.[1]

In Chapter 4, we used a balanced panel of 319 firms for the analysis after eliminating firms which changed their accounting year during the sample period (1982-1991) or had a missing year or values. For the analysis of this chapter, we did not require the panel to be balanced. However, we further eliminated observations if any of the measure of investment, sales or capital stock at replacement cost had increased or decreased by a factor of three or more, since we might not expect the same dynamic adjustment process to characterise these large changes. Extreme outlying values of the variables used in regressions also resulted in an observation being deleted from the sample, as detailed in the Data Appendix. The removal of these outliers left an unbalanced sample of 367 manufacturing firms with at least six consecutive annual observations between 1982 and 1991. In this chapter, we use this data set to estimate an accelerator model, error correction model and Euler equation model of company investment.

For the estimation of a Q model, which requires share price information, we constructed a second data set which includes the stock market valuation for these firms. As we noted in Chapter 4, our original data included some observations on firms before they were listed on the stock market. For this reason, to estimate the Q model, we have to exclude observations for which no share price data was available. This process left 196 manufacturing firms with at least six observations including their stock market valuation.

The main complexity in constructing this data set for our Q model came from the need to match the accounting data with information on share prices and the number of shares outstanding, because the stock market data came from a different source.[2] We had first to match the different company codes between these two data sources. As the two different data sources did not share the same company code, this matching process involved the manual collation of the companies by consulting the 'Handbook of Korean listed companies' published by Daewoo Securities annually. It should also be noted that as data from the end of the previous year's accounts are required to calculate the Q ratio, the time period available for the Q model is 1983-1991.

The main data requirements for estimating the models in this chapter are the ratio of investment to the current-cost capital stock, and a measure of tax-adjusted Q. Investment has been measured as the difference between additions to the stock of tangible fixed assets and disposals of tangible fixed assets, both obtained from the flow of funds statement. Calculating the current-cost capital stock and measuring Q are quite complex and potentially problematic tasks. As for the current-cost capital stock, we used a standard perpetual inventory method, except that Korean accounts report the most recent year in which assets were revalued on the balance sheet, and we used this information to construct the benchmark. We then assume that in the most recent revaluation year the book value of the stock of tangible fixed assets is the same as the current cost capital stock, and calculate the capital stock for both earlier and later years using the investment data, inflation rates and depreciation rates.The details of this calculation and the construction of a measure of tax-adjusted Q are given in the Data Appendix.

With these two main data sets, we estimated our investment models for both the whole sample and for sub-samples according to the sample separation criteria described in the introduction to this chapter. The precise definitions of these separation criteria are also detailed in the Data Appendix.

6.3 Econometric methods for panel data

The objective of this section is to explain the various estimators which we use in this chapter to estimate investment models from company panel data. While panel data give us richer information than aggregate time-series or single cross section data, estimation is more complicated.

In our study, panel data obtained from the company accounts of Korean manufacturing firms is used to estimate investment models in order to investigate the sensitivity of investment to financial constraints. The typical investment models we estimate take the following form:

$$y_{it} = \beta\, y_{i,t-1} + \gamma\, x_{it} + \alpha_t + \alpha_i + v_{it} \qquad (6.1)$$

where the subscript i refers to the company (i = 1,2, ... ,N) and the subscript t refers to the time period (t = 2,3, ... ,T). The error term contains unobserved company-specific effects α_i, and time-specific effects α_t, as well as idiosyncratic time-varying shocks v_{it}. The v_{it} are assumed to be independently distributed across individuals with zero mean, but arbitrary forms of heteroskedasticity across companies and time are allowed. The data we are using is a panel of company accounts with a large number of companies ($N \approx 400$), but covering a short time period ($T \leq 10$).

It is noteworthy that equation (6.1) has a dynamic specification, in that the lagged value of the dependent variable is included as a regressor. As we reviewed in Chapter 5, this dynamic structure is a feature of several leading models of company investment.

Three estimators will be discussed here and used in the following empirical sections: the OLS levels estimator; the Within Groups estimator; and the Generalised Method of Moments (GMM) first-differenced estimator.

Consistent estimation of the parameters of interest β and γ with these estimators in short T panels depends on what can be assumed about correlated individual effects and endogenous regressors. Three key issues are the covariance between x_{it} and α_i, the covariance between x_{it} and v_{it} and the serial correlation of v_{it}. It is important to note that $y_{i,t-1}$ and α_i are necessarily correlated in the dynamic setting if firm-specific effects are present, and that $y_{i,t-1}$ is necessarily correlated with $v_{i,t-1}$.

The simplest way to estimate (6.1) is OLS estimation in levels. In a pure static model without the lagged dependent variable, the OLS estimator is consistent if the regressor x_{it} is uncorrelated with the individual effect α_i and strictly exogenous with respect to v_{it}, irrespective of whether the v_{it} are serially correlated or not.[3] But in the dynamic model, as the lagged dependent variable is correlated with the individual effect, the OLS estimator in levels is likely to produce an upwards biased estimate of β.

The standard response to correlation between individual effects and regressors in the static panel data literature is the Within Groups estimator. The idea of this estimator is first to eliminate the individual effects from the error term by subtracting group means from each observation.[4] In the pure static model, if the regressor is correlated with the individual effect but strictly exogenous with respect to v_{it}, the Within Groups estimator is consistent. But, in the dynamic specification, the lagged dependent variable is not strictly exogenous, due to the correlation between $y_{i,t-1}$ and $v_{i,t-1}$. The Within Groups estimator is likely to produce a downwards biased estimate of β, due to the resulting correlation between transformed $y_{i,t-1}$ and transformed v_{it} in short T panels (see Nickell 1981).

As seen above, in dynamic specifications with lagged dependent variables, neither OLS in levels nor the Within Groups estimator is consistent in short T panels. This result holds irrespective of the assumption about the correlation between the regressor x_{it} and the individual effects or the idiosyncratic error term. That is, the assumption that $cov(x_{it},v_{is}) = 0$ and $cov(x_{it},\alpha_i) = 0$ does not guarantee the consistency of OLS and Within Groups estimators in the dynamic specification of the model. However it is interesting to note that the biases for β are likely to be in opposite directions, suggesting upper and lower bounds on the true value of this parameter.

Other than the obvious disadvantage of the above estimators, the assumption that x_{it} is strictly exogenous with respect to v_{is} is not attractive in the present application, in view of the underlying theory of the investment models. For example, current values of cash flow and Tobin's Q are likely to be correlated with current shocks to investment. We require a consistent estimator for dynamic models that can allow for correlation between the regressor and the individual effect, and for correlation between the regressor and disturbances v_{it}.

Holtz-Eakin, Newey and Rosen (1988) and Arellano and Bond (1991) developed Generalized Method of Moments (GMM) estimators for dynamic panel data models that have these properties. The basic idea is to eliminate the individual effects by taking first differences of the model, and then to use lagged variables as instruments. The method extends the instrumental variables estimators proposed by Anderson and Hsiao (1982), and relies on limited serial correlation in v_{it} to obtain valid instruments. The advantage of the GMM estimator is that it optimally exploits all the (linear) moment restrictions specified by the model. In particular, more lagged instruments become available for the differenced equations as we consider later cross-sections of the panel.

If we take the first difference of equation (6.1), we obtain

$$\Delta y_{it} = \beta \, \Delta y_{i,t-1} + \gamma \, \Delta x_{it} + \Delta\alpha_t + \Delta v_{it}. \qquad (6.2)$$

The effect of first differencing is to eliminate the individual effects and to introduce a first-order moving average error term Δv_{it}. Suppose for illustration that v_{it} is serially uncorrelated, and that x_{it}

is endogenous (correlated with v_{it}). We can then use a different number of lagged instruments for both x and y in different time periods. For t=3, equation (6.2) becomes (omitting time-specific effects for simplicity),[5]

$$y_{i3} - y_{i2} = \beta(y_{i2} - y_{i1}) + \gamma(x_{i3} - x_{i2}) + (v_{i3} - v_{i2}). \tag{6.3}$$

Here y_{i1} and x_{i1} are available as instruments for $(y_{i2} - y_{i1})$ and $(x_{i3} - x_{i2})$, as they are correlated with the regressors but are not correlated with the error term. For t=4, there are 4 instruments available $(y_{i1}, y_{i2}, x_{i1}, x_{i2})$ for $(y_{i3} - y_{i2})$ and $(x_{i4} - x_{i3})$, and so on until the last equation when we have 2(T-2) instruments available $(y_{i1}, y_{i2}, \ldots, y_{i,T-2}, x_{i1}, x_{i2}, \ldots, x_{i,T-2})$.

The number of valid instruments available in each equation differs according to the correlation between x_{it} and v_{it}, and according to the serial correlation of v_{it}. For example, if x_{it} is predetermined with respect to v_{it}, rather than endogenous, but v_{it} is again serially uncorrelated, then the set of instruments available in the first-differenced equation for period t becomes $(y_{i1}, y_{i2}, \ldots, y_{i,t-2}, x_{i1}, x_{i2}, \ldots, x_{i,t-1})$. Furthermore if x_{it} is strictly exogenous with respect to v_{it} then this set becomes $(y_{i1}, y_{i2}, \ldots, y_{i,t-2}, x_{i1}, x_{i2}, \ldots, x_{iT})$. Conversely if x_{it} is endogenous but v_{it} is an MA(1) disturbance, then the set of instruments available in period t becomes $(y_{i1}, y_{i2}, \ldots, y_{i,t-3}, x_{i1}, x_{i2}, \ldots, x_{i,t-3})$. Hence it is important to test the validity of the instruments used to ensure that we obtain consistent estimates.

Provided that v_{it} is serially uncorrelated, Δv_{it} is a first-order moving average process. So we should observe significantly negative first-order serial correlation in Δv_{it} but negligible second-order serial correlation in Δv_{it} if this assumption is correct. Only then are lagged endogenous variables dated t-2 valid instruments. To test the validity of this assumption we test for the presence of second-order serial correlation in the GMM residuals using the one degree of freedom test proposed by Arellano and Bond (1991). We also report Sargan tests of the over-identifying restrictions exploited as an additional test of instrument validity.

Further details of the GMM estimator and test statistics we use can be found in Arellano and Bond (1991). In Monte Carlo simulations these authors found that this GMM estimator provides significant improvements in precision compared to simpler instrumental variables estimators. This estimation procedure was carried out on a microcomputer using GAUSS 3.1 and the DPD program (see Arellano and Bond 1988).

As our panel data covers many heterogeneous firms and several time periods, the disturbances v_{it} are likely to be heteroskedastic. The DPD program produces both one-step and two-step GMM estimators, the latter using the one-step residuals to form the asymptotically optimal weighting matrix. While there is no gain from using the two-step estimator in the homoskedastic case, the two-step estimator is asymptotically more efficient if the error term is heteroskedastic. However, it has been found in simulations that the asymptotic standard errors for the two-step estimator can be seriously misleading in small samples, particularly in the presence of heteroskedasticity (see Arellano and Bond 1991, Blundell and Bond 1995). As this problem appeared to be present in our empirical results, we report the one-step estimates for which inference is more reliable.

6.4 Testing investment models using Korean company accounts data

A sales-accelerator model

Model Based on our discussion in Chapter 5, an accelerator model can be specified as follows:

$$\left(\frac{I_{it}}{K_{i,t-1}}\right) = \beta_0 + \beta_1\left(\frac{I_{i,t-1}}{K_{i,t-2}}\right) + \beta_2\left(\frac{Y_{it}}{K_{i,t-1}}\right) + \beta_3\left(\frac{Y_{i,t-1}}{K_{i,t-2}}\right) + e_{it} \qquad (6.4)$$

for i= 1,2, ... ,N and t= 3,4, ... ,T. Here, I is investment, K is the capital stock at replacement cost and Y is sales, which is used as a proxy for output.

The disturbance term e_{it} is assumed to have the following structure:

$$e_{it} = \alpha_i + \alpha_t + v_{it}, \tag{6.5}$$

that is, the error term may contain company-specific effects α_i and time-specific effects α_t, as well as an idiosyncratic shock v_{it}. In equation (6.4), the lagged value of the dependent variable, $\left(\frac{I_{i,t-1}}{K_{i,t-2}}\right)$, has been included to allow the possibility that dynamics are required in accelerator specifications to reflect slow adjustment of the actual capital stock to the desired capital stock. In estimating equation (6.4), We will later include a cash flow term, $\left(\frac{CF_{it}}{K_{i,t-1}}\right)$, and its lagged value to test whether equation (6.4) is mis-specified. Cash flow is measured by adding back depreciation charges to a measure of profit after interest, tax and preference dividends, as described in the Data Appendix.

Empirical results for the whole sample Table 6.1 presents estimation results for our sample of 367 Korean manufacturing companies using the various estimators which were explained in the previous section. The OLS estimator uses the levels form of equation (6.4), the Within Groups estimator uses deviations from group means, and the GMM estimator uses the first differences of equation (6.4). In column (i), OLS is applied to the dynamic specification of the accelerator model in levels. The coefficient on the lagged dependent variable is 0.41, and we find significant effects from the sales terms. In column (ii), we present Within Groups estimates of the same specification. Here the coefficient on the lagged dependent variable falls to 0.067.

In column (iii), we present our basic GMM results for the same specification, using instruments dated t-2 and earlier.[6] The coefficient on the lagged dependent variable is 0.14, which lies between the corresponding OLS and Within Groups estimates. Recall that the OLS levels estimate is likely to be biased upwards in the presence of firm-specific effects, whilst the Within Groups estimate is likely to be biased downward. These biases appear to be important, so we will concentrate on the GMM results. The Sargan test does not reject the validity of the instruments used. The m_2 statistic does not reject the hypothesis of no second-order serial correlation in the differenced residuals, which allows the use of the t-2 instrument set to deal with the endogeneity of the regressors. The m_1 statistic does show significant negative first-order serial correlation in the differenced residuals, Δv_{it}, which is expected if the levels residuals v_{it} are serially uncorrelated. Again we find evidence of dynamics in the equation, and a significant effect from current sales.

In columns (iv-v), we include additional cash flow variables to test this basic specification of the investment equation.[7] In column (iv), we use both current and lagged cash flow. Cash flow is found to have a positive effect on investment, and the two cash flow terms are jointly significant at the 10 % level. As the lagged term is individually insignificant, we drop it in column (v). We then find the coefficient on current cash flow is more significant, with a t-statistic of 2.24. Note that in contrast to some previous studies, cash flow is here treated as an endogenous variable in the investment equation. Also in this specification, the Sargan and m_2 statistics do not reject the validity of the instruments used.

This sensitivity of investment to cash flow for Korean companies is in line with the findings of several previous studies including Fazzari, Hubbard and Petersen (1988) for US companies; Blundell, Bond, Devereux and Schiantarelli (1992) and Devereux and Schiantarelli (1990) for UK companies; and Hayashi and Inoue (1991) and Hoshi, Kashyap and Scharfstein (1991) for Japanese companies. As we discussed in Chapter 5, there may be two reasons for this sensitivity in the context of the accelerator model. First, if the assumption of a perfect capital market is not correct, the investment model becomes mis-specified. In this case, the positive effect of cash flow may be due to the presence of financial constraints on investment, such as those implied by the hierarchy of finance model. Second, the 'ad hoc' character of the accelerator model implies that the cash flow variable may also be significant if cash flow provides additional information about expected demand that is not captured by the output (sales) variable. Whether the significance of cash flow is due to expectations or financial constraints is not established by estimating the accelerator model with the whole sample.

This issue will now be further investigated. As we reviewed in Chapter 5, several related studies have addressed this question by dividing the total sample of companies into sub-samples, and estimating separate models for each group. We will also divide our total sample into sub-samples, and investigate whether significant coefficient differences are found for different types of firms. The specification in column (v) will be used as the prototype.

Empirical results for the sub-samples In this section, our sample of firms has been disaggregated (pairwise) into sub-samples according to the five criteria that were used in Chapter 4. These are group affiliation, size, export ratio, age and heavy/light industries. All coefficients in the estimated models, including those on the time dummies, are allowed to take different values in the two parts of the sample, by interacting these terms with a zero/one dummy variable (D_i). Lagged values of the interactions are included in the instrument set, so that this is equivalent to estimating the model separately for the two sub-samples.

Table 6.2 presents the results of estimating the above accelerator model with these five divisions of the sample. In column (i), the dummy variable D_i is zero for firms that are affiliated to a Chaebol group, and D_i is one for non-group firms. The first four coefficients therefore relate to the sub-sample where the accelerator model is estimated for the group-affiliated firms, while the remaining coefficients estimate the *difference* of the coefficients on each variable between the group-affiliated sub-sample and the non-group sub-sample. To obtain the accelerator model coefficients for non group-affiliated firms, we must add together the first set and second set of reported coefficients. For example, the coefficient on the lagged dependent variable for non-group firms is 0.23 - 0.15 = 0.08.

In column (i) of Table 6.2 we can formally test the null hypothesis that parameters are constant between group-affiliated firms and non group-affiliated firms. First the current sales variable is significant for group-affiliated firms with a t-statistic of 5.01, and the corresponding coefficient difference between the two sub-samples is also significant with a t-statistic of 3.09. The effect of sales on investment is much weaker for the non-group firms. Second, there is a large and significant difference in the coefficient on the cash flow variable across the sub-samples. For group firms, there is no significant effect of cash flow on investment. In contrast, the coefficient on cash flow for non-group firms is 0.45 (0.53 - 0.08), and the null hypothesis that this coefficient is common for the two sub-samples is rejected with a t-statistic of 2.29. The significance of these coefficient differences between group firms and non-group firms is confirmed by the joint test, which has a p-value of 0.018. The m_2 statistic (-0.77) is consistent with our use of t-2 instruments and the Sargan test of over-identifying restrictions is also acceptable. Overall, these results are consistent with the view that the significance of the cash flow term in our accelerator model reflects financial constraints rather than expectation-formation, and that financial constraints on investment are more important for firms in Korea that are not affiliated to Chaebol groups.

In column (ii), we present the results when the total sample is divided according to firm size. The dummy variable D_i takes the value zero for firms with more than 1000 employees, and one otherwise. The first four coefficients therefore relate to the larger firms. Note that adjustment of the capital stock is slower for the larger firms (i.e. investment is more persistent), as indicated by the significantly lower coefficient on the lagged dependent variable for the smaller firms.

However, the other coefficients are not significantly different between large and small firms, including that on cash flow.

Column (iii) presents the results when the total sample is divided according to the firm's export ratio. The dummy variable D_i is zero for firms whose ratio of exports to total sales is greater than 30 %, and one otherwise. The first four coefficients therefore relate to the more export oriented firms. We do not find any significant coefficient differences between these two sub-samples, according to either the individual or joint tests of significance. The remaining two columns present the results from the division of our sample by age and industry classification. These results do not indicate any significant differences in investment behaviour between old and young firms and between heavy industries and light industries, and do not suggest any difference in the impact of financial constraints on investment between these sub-samples.

An error correction model

Model The version of Bean (1981)'s error correction model of investment we consider here is

$$\left(\frac{I_{it}}{K_{i,t-1}}\right) = \beta_0 + \beta_1\left(\frac{I_{i,t-1}}{K_{i,t-2}}\right) + \beta_2\Delta y_{it} + \beta_3(k - y)_{i,t-1} + e_{it} \qquad (6.6)$$

for i= 1,2, ... ,N and t= 3,4, ... ,T. Here, I is investment, K is the capital stock at replacement cost, y is the log of sales (Y) and k is the log of the capital stock (K). We do not attempt to measure the user cost of capital explicitly, but by allowing for unobserved firm effects and time effects it is hoped that we control for most of the variation in the user cost.

The error term e_{it} is assumed to have the same structure described in equation (6.5). In this model the capital stock adjusts to correct past deviations from the desired level, provided the coefficient β_3 on the error correction term is negative. The proportionality imposed in equation (6.6) depends on constant returns to scale, and will be tested. Additional cash flow terms will again be included to test this specification.

Empirical results for the whole sample Table 6.3 presents the results of estimating the error correction model in equation (6.6) for our sample of 367 Korean manufacturing companies, using the three estimators described previously. In column (i), OLS is applied to the dynamic form of the model in levels. The coefficient on the lagged dependent variable is 0.24 with high statistical significance. In column (ii), we present Within Groups estimates of the same specification and observe that the coefficient on the lagged dependent variable falls to 0.07. In column (iii), we present our basic GMM results for the same specification, using instruments dated t-2 and earlier. The finding that the coefficient on the lagged dependent variable is between these two estimates, and significantly lower than the OLS estimate, is consistent with our results for the accelerator model, and again indicates the presence of firm-specific effects.

The basic GMM results for this model in column (iii) appear quite satisfactory. The error correction term is correctly signed and statistically significant: a capital stock above the long-run desired level is associated with lower investment, and vice-versa. We tested the assumption of constant returns to scale by including an additional $y_{i,t-1}$ term, which relaxes the restriction of proportionality imposed in column (iii). The coefficient on this extra term was insignificantly different from zero, suggesting that constant returns to scale is an acceptable restriction to impose in the long-run. The serial correlation test does not indicate significant second-order autocorrelation in the residuals. The Sargan statistic is quite marginal, although the validity of the instruments used is not rejected at the conventional 5 % level. However, some indication of mis-specification would not be surprising if important cash flow effects are omitted from this model, and/or if coefficients should be allowed to vary across group and non-group firms. We now investigate if this is the case.

In column (iv) we proceed to add cash flow terms to our basic model. We initially include both current and lagged cash flow terms. The form of the cash flow variable is the same as used in the accelerator model. The current term is again positive and more significant than the lagged term, although the joint test suggests the cash flow terms have only weak statistical significance in this model. In column (v) we drop the lagged cash flow term. The current cash flow term remains positive, with a t-statistic of 1.5. Note also that the validity of the instruments used becomes less marginal according to the Sargan test when this cash flow term is included.

The sensitivity of investment to cash flow in this model could again be explained either as the result of financial constraints or as the result of an expectations-formation process that is not fully captured in the basic specification. This issue will be further investigated by examining the results from the sub-samples.

Empirical results for the sub-samples In this section, we will divide our sample of firms into two according to the same criteria used for the accelerator model. The same method is used to formally test parameter constancy across these sub-samples.

In column (i) of Table 6.4, we allow the coefficients in the model to vary between group-affiliated firms and non group-affiliated firms. The most interesting result is again what happens to the coefficient on the cash flow term. As we found for the accelerator model, there is no indication that the investment of group firms is sensitive to cash flow: the point estimate for group firms is actually negative. For non-group firms there is again a large positive coefficient on cash flow, and the difference in the estimated coefficient between these two sub-samples has a t-value of 1.74, which is significant at the 10 % level. However the remaining coefficients in the model are found to be similar, and the joint test of parameter constancy reflects this.

In the other classifications, we do not find significant differences in the estimated coefficients, although there is a weak indication that cash flow may matter more in the investment decisions of smaller firms, young firms and firms in heavy industry. Also we again find the coefficient on the lagged dependent variable to be lower in the case of smaller companies.

An Euler equation model

Model and data The Euler equation specification we consider is similar to that used by Bond and Meghir (1994a), and has the form

$$(I/K)_{it} = \beta_1 (I/K)_{i,t-1} + \beta_2 (I/K)^2_{i,t-1} + \beta_3 (\Pi/K)_{i,t-1} + \beta_4 (Y/K)_{i,t-1} + e_{it} \qquad (6.7$$

for i= 1,2, ... ,N and t= 2,3, ... ,T. Here, I is investment, K is the capital stock at replacement cost, Y is sales and Π is gross operating profit.

The error term e_{it} is assumed to have the same structure described in equation (6.5). We again assume that time-specific effects and firm-specific effects control adequately for the variation in the user cost of capital.

We used the same sample here as for the previous models. Investment again measures additions to tangible fixed assets net of disposals of tangible fixed assets. The current cost capital stock is calculated in the same way and described in the Data Appendix.

However, it should be noted that the investment rate modelled here is the ratio of investment to the *end of period* capital stock, and a different method is used to calculate the ratios of gross operating profit and sales to capital stock.

First, the measure of gross operating profit differs from the cash flow measure used in the previous sections. This reflects the different role played by this variable in the Euler equation. Cash flow variables were added to the accelerator and error correction models simply to test the basic econometric specifications. But as explained in Chapter 5, under constant returns to scale the ratio of gross operating profit to capital appears in the Euler equation as a measure of the marginal profitability of capital, even under the null hypothesis of no financial constraints. While we measured cash flow in the accelerator model and error correction model as profit after tax, interest and preference dividends plus the provision for depreciation of fixed assets, in the Euler equation model, the measure of profit we use is gross operating profit before deducting tax, interest and preference dividends, as well as depreciation.

Secondly, while previously we simply used the ratios of nominal cash flow and sales to the beginning of period capital stock, in this model we applied some price adjustments to be consistent with the theoretical specification. If $P_t\Pi_t$ denotes the nominal value of gross operating profit and $P^I_tK_t$ denotes the nominal value of the end of period capital stock at replacement cost, we construct

$$\left(\frac{\Pi}{K}\right)_t = \left(\frac{P_t\Pi_t}{P^I_tK_t}\right)\frac{P^I_t}{P_t} \qquad (6.8)$$

where P^I_t is the investment goods price, for which we used the wholesale price index for investment goods; and P_t is the output price, for which we used the wholesale price index for all industry. The ratio of real output to end of period capital stock is constructed in the same way, using sales as a proxy for the nominal value of output.

One consequence of these differences is that we have one extra year of data available to estimate the Euler equation model.

Empirical results for the whole sample We first estimate equation (6.7) by OLS, Within Groups and GMM, using the whole sample of 367 companies. Table 6.5 reports estimates of the basic Euler equation specification from these estimators. First, comparison between the coefficients on the lagged dependent variable from the three estimators shows that as expected the GMM estimate in column (iii) lies between the OLS and Within Groups estimates. Biases from correlated firm-specific effects again appear to be important in this model.

In view of the fact that the theoretical derivation of this model suggests we should find $\beta_1 > 1$, $\beta_2 < -1$, $\beta_3 < 0$ and $\beta_4 \geq 0$, the estimated coefficients are not satisfactory, although they all have the expected signs except the coefficient on gross operating profit. Although there is no evidence of significant second-order serial correlation in the residuals, the Sargan test of over-identifying restrictions rejects the validity of the instrument set used in column (iii).

We also estimate the model using the GMM estimator in first differences but excluding the instruments from period t-2. This was found to give a significant improvement in the UK results presented by Bond and Meghir (1994a). Our results are reported in column (iv). The main effect is that the coefficient estimates become very imprecise. However the estimates in column (iv) are significantly different from those in column (iii) according to both Hausman test and Sargan difference test comparisons, and the Sargan test does not reject the validity of the instruments used in column (iv).[8] Thus we reject the validity of instruments dated t-2, but do not obtain any more satisfactory parameter estimates when these are excluded.

Although the results of estimating the Euler equation model using the whole sample are rather disappointing in general, it is notable that the coefficient on gross operating profit consistently has a positive sign, contrary to the prediction of the theoretical model in the absence of financial constraints. According to the theoretical derivation, this term reflects the marginal revenue product of capital and should enter this specification of the Euler equation with a negative sign. However, this result has been derived only under the assumption that the firm can raise as much finance for investment as it desires at a given real opportunity cost. If this assumption is incorrect then the profit term could reflect an influence from financial constraints in addition to marginal profitability.

In the previous sections, we have presented evidence that models imposing common coefficients for all firms in the sample are mis-specified, and that the investment of non-group affiliated firms may be significantly affected by the presence of financial constraints. In the next section we investigate this further in the context of the Euler equation model.

Empirical results for the sub-samples To test whether financial constraints affect the investment decisions of Korean manufacturing firms, we divide the sample according to the five criteria used previously and outlined in the Data Appendix.

First, we divide the sample into group-affiliated and non group-affiliated firms. Note that instruments from period t-2 are not included in the instrument set used here. In Table 6.6, column (i) presents the results from this division. The first four coefficients relate to the Euler equation estimated only for group-affiliated firms, and the second four coefficients estimate parameter differences between the two sub-samples.

If we first consider the Wald statistic which tests the joint significance of the coefficient differences between these two sub-samples, the p-value of 0.00 strongly rejects the null hypothesis that these parameters are constant across the two sub-samples. The most significant differences are found for the lagged dependent variable and the squared investment term. The difference of the coefficients on the lagged dependent variable is significant with a t-statistic of -4.28, while that on the squared investment term has a t-statistic of 4.26. It is striking that the estimated coefficients for group firms are quite similar to the parameters for the Euler equation suggested by the adjustment costs theory in the absence of financial constraints. The estimate of β_1(0.80) is not significantly different from 1 and the estimate of β_2(-1.70) is not significantly different from -1. In contrast, in the results for non-group firms, β_1 becomes negative (0.80 - 1.15 = -0.35) and β_2 becomes positive (2.09 - 1.70 = 0.39), and neither estimate for the non-group firms is significantly different from zero. The investment dynamics thus appear to be consistent with an adjustment costs model with no financial constraints for the group-affiliated firms, but inconsistent with this model for the non-group firms. The estimated coefficient on the gross operating profits term is not significantly positive for the group firms, and overall our estimates for this sub-sample are rather similar to the results for the UK companies identified as not affected by financial constraints in Bond and Meghir (1994a).

Column (ii) presents the results with sub-samples divided by size. The first four coefficients relate to firms with more than 1000 employees. The p-value of the joint Wald test is 0.183, which does not reject the hypothesis of constant parameters across the two sub-samples. Here the basic Euler equation does not characterise well the investment data in either sub-sample, which is consistent with the presence of financially-constrained non-group affiliated companies in both sub-samples. There is however a weak indication that the gross operating profit variable has a different effect on the smaller companies (t-statistic = 1.56).

The only significant difference we find in the remaining divisions of the full sample relates to the coefficient on the lagged dependent variable for firms established after 1960. For none of these sub-samples is the investment data consistent with the basic Euler equation specification.

A Q model

Model The basic Q model of investment, as explained in Chapter 5, can be written as follows:

$$(I/K)_{it} = \beta Q_{it} + \alpha_t + \alpha_i + v_{it} \tag{6.9}$$

As noted by Blundell, Bond, Devereux and Schiantarelli (1992), if the adjustment cost shocks v_{it} follow an AR(1) process, this will imply a dynamic specification with additional terms in $Q_{i,t-1}$ and $(I/K)_{i,t-1}$, subject to the common factor restriction. In this section we will estimate the above basic equation and variants using company accounts data for Korean manufacturing firms. The Q variable in equation (6.9) is tax-adjusted Q, the construction of which is described in the Data Appendix, and the components of the error term have already been explained above. Without repeating the theoretical details of the Q model, in the next sections we will describe the data requirements for this model and the empirical results.

Data Unlike the other investment models we estimate, the Q model cannot be estimated using all the observations in our data set. As was noted in Chapter 4, the data includes not only observations after the stock market listing of the company, but also observations dating back up to 5 years prior to the listing if these are available. Because it is necessary to use share prices to calculate Q, only the observations after each firm's listing on the stock market can be used. Thus the data set used here covers only the 196 manufacturing companies for which at least six observations after listing were available. We again deleted observations in which exceptionally large changes in the capital stock at replacement cost, investment or sales were observed, since we might not expect the quadratic adjustment cost function to characterise these adjustments well. The precise selection criteria used are detailed in the Data Appendix.

The observations included in the data we use to estimate the Q model are therefore a strict subset of the sample used in the preceding sections. To confirm that the observations in this data set do not show significantly different investment behaviour, we re-estimated the accelerator model, error correction model and Euler equation model using only this subset of the data. The results were very similar to those reported previously.

Empirical results for the whole sample Table 6.7 presents the estimates of equation (6.9) from three estimators: OLS levels, Within Groups and GMM in first differences. Both OLS and Within Groups estimators indicate a positive and significant relationship between investment and Q, but only provide consistent parameter estimates if Q_{it} is uncorrelated with v_{it}, which is inconsistent with the Q theory. The serial correlation tests in all three cases indicate dynamic mis-specification, which results in invalid instruments and biased parameter estimates when the differenced GMM estimator is used. This is confirmed by the Sargan statistic in column (iii). The explanatory power of the static OLS model is also very low.

In columns (i-iii) of Table 6.8, we present the results from these three estimators for a more general dynamic specification than equation (6.9), in which both lagged Q and the lagged dependent variable are included. Although the GMM estimates (column (iii)) of the coefficients on the Q terms are much less precise than the other estimators, it is interesting to note that both the m_2 statistic and the Sargan test become more acceptable in this dynamic specification. The fact that the coefficient on the lagged dependent variable is very significant, and the m_2 statistic is acceptably low, is consistent with the error v_{it} in the basic model of equation (6.9) being AR(1). This dynamic specification can be formally tested against the pure static model by testing the implied 'common factor' restriction. Although this would not be rejected here, this is due to the striking insignificance of both Q variables in these results, which is not very encouraging. From Table 6.8 we also find that the OLS estimate of the coefficient on the lagged dependent variable is biased upward, showing evidence of firm-specific effects. As would also be expected, the Within Groups estimate in column (ii) produces a downward bias on this coefficient.

In column (iv), we use the same dynamic specification but here assume that Q is strictly exogenous with respect to v_{it}. Under this assumption, the past, current and future observations on Q are available as instruments. The coefficients on the Q terms are larger and more significant than in column (iii), where we allow Q to be endogenous. The coefficient on Q_{it} is significant, with a t-statistic of 2.28. But, unlike in column (iii), the evidence from the specification test statistics is somewhat conflicting. While the m_2 statistic does not show significant evidence of second-order serial correlation, the Sargan statistic suggests that the validity of this instrument set is very marginal. This would be consistent with the possibility of contemporaneous correlation between Q_{it} and v_{it}.

As we noted in Chapter 5, we should allow Q to be endogenous to be consistent with the Q theory. On theoretical grounds the GMM estimator in column (iii) should therefore be preferred. As the instrument set used in column (iii) is a strict sub-set of that used in column (iv), we can formally compare these estimates using a Sargan difference test. The value of 45.56 ($\chi^2(29)$) has a p-value of 0.03, which rejects the validity of the extra instruments used in column (iv). Further analysis will rely on the specification and instrument set in column (iii).

As we observed in the previous chapter, in deriving the basic Q model, strong assumptions on the product market, technology, adjustment costs and stock market efficiency were required for average Q to be a sufficient statistic for marginal Q. In particular, perfect competition, linear homogeneous technology and a strongly efficient stock market were required. If these assumptions are not valid, it is expected that financial variables such as cash flow and output variables could play a part in explaining investment, as has been found in applications of the Q model to aggregate time series data. As has been pointed out by Fazzari, Hubbard and Petersen (1988), if some firms find it difficult or costly to raise external finance, their investment could be affected by the availability of internal finance. We investigate this possibility by adding cash flow and sales variables to the dynamic specification of the Q model. The cash flow term is defined here as cash flow *net of tax, interest and preference dividends*, as a proportion of *end of period* capital stock at replacement cost (denoted $(CF/K)_{it}$). Similarly sales are expressed as a proportion of the end of period capital stock.

In Table 6.9 we present the results from models which include these extra variables. Column (i) repeats the basic specification for ease of comparison. In column (ii), we add a cash flow term and estimate the model treating $(CF/K)_{it}$ as endogenous and correlated with the firm-specific effects. Current cash flow was found to be insignificant and dropped from the specification, and only lagged cash flow is therefore included. This cash flow term has a positive effect on investment and is statistically significant, with a t-statistic of 2.57. The Q terms remain insignificantly different from zero. However the Sargan and m_2 statistics do not suggest the invalidity of instruments or mis-specification of the model.

The final column of Table 6.9 investigates the effect of including additional terms in the ratio of sales to end of period capital stock, denoted $(Y/K)_{it}$. We used both current and lagged sales terms in the estimation and they were both found to be significant. The coefficient on cash flow falls a little but remains positive and statistically significant. The negative coefficient on current output may reflect imperfect competition in product markets, as suggested by Hayashi (1982) and Schiantarelli and Georgoutsos (1990). However, both m_2 and Sargan statistics cast doubt on the validity of the instruments used in this specification. We will use the specification in column (ii) as a prototype to further investigate the effect of financial constraints on investment, using sub-samples of this data set, in the next section.

Empirical results using the sub-samples In this section, we divide our sample of firms into sub-samples in the same way as described for the previous models, and test the hypothesis of parameter constancy between these sub-samples.

In column (i) of Table 6.10, we test the null that the parameters are constant between group-affiliated firms and non-group-affiliated firms. As before, the first four coefficients relate to group firms, while the last four coefficients estimate parameter differences between the two sub-samples. The most interesting difference between the two sub-samples again relates to the cash flow variable. The coefficient on cash flow for group firms is 0.01, whilst for non-group firms it is 0.25. Although the t-statistic associated with this coefficient difference is only 1.3, this difference in the effect of cash flow on the investment spending of group firms and non-group firms is very much in line with our previous findings. It is also noteworthy that the Q ratio, particularly $Q_{i,t-1}$, is more informative for the group firms than for the non-group firms.

Interestingly, in these results for the Q model we find that the differences in coefficients between small firms and large firms are more significant than those between group firms and non-group firms. Cash flow has a positive and statistically significant effect on investment for the smaller companies but not for the larger companies. The t-statistic associated with this coefficient difference is 2.32, and the joint test also indicates significant parameter differences. We also find that *changes* in Q appear to affect the investment decisions of smaller firms, although it is not clear how this result should be interpreted. On the whole, the above results are again consistent with the view that the significance of the cash flow term in our basic Q model reflects financial constraints rather than expectation-formation, and that financial constraints on investment are more important for smaller firms and the firms in Korea that are not affiliated to Chaebol groups.

Columns (iii-v) list the results from the division of our sample by export ratio, age and heavy/light industries respectively. We note that financial constraints on investment appear to be marginally more important for domestically oriented firms, and for firms operating in heavy industries.

6.5 Summary and discussion of empirical results

In section 6.4, we presented the results of our econometric analysis in which we tested a range of investment models using the company accounts data of Korean manufacturing firms. The main objective of the study was to investigate whether the investment spending of Korean firms is affected by financial constraints; and, if this is the case, whether the impact of financial constraints is consistent with a 'hierarchy of finance' explanation based on external finance being relatively expensive for certain types of firms. This task was carried out by estimating a range of investment models: a sales-accelerator model, an error correction model, a Q model and an Euler equation model.[9]

Throughout the analysis, cash flow was used as our main financial variable.

Our basic format of estimation was divided into two stages.

We first estimated the investment models using the whole sample of 367 companies, except for the Q model in which we could only use 196 companies. Using the econometric methods set out in section 6.3, we began the empirical analysis by investigating the preferred specifications and estimators. Overall, the GMM estimator was preferred because our results indicated the presence of unobserved firm-specific effects. We then added a financial variable, cash flow, to the models - except in the Euler equation model in which a similar financial variable is already incorporated in the basic specification. The coefficient on this additional cash flow term was generally positive and significant. As far as the other regressors were concerned, for the accelerator and error correction models, the sales terms were significant and dynamics were also found to be important. For the Q model, the performance of our measure of Q was disappointing, and the coefficients in the Euler equation model were estimated very imprecisely.

The evidence on the effect of cash flow was certainly consistent with the possibility of financial constraints, but we must be cautious in drawing this conclusion. Especially for the accelerator and error correction models, it is not clear from these full sample results whether the significant effect of cash flow reflects the effect of financial constraints on investment, or whether information on cash flow merely helps to forecast expected future demand.

This motivated the second stage of our econometric study, using sub-samples of the data set. We used five different criteria to divide the sample into two parts. These were group affiliation, size of the firm, export ratio, age and industry classification. We tested the null hypothesis that the parameters of our investment models were constant across these sub-samples.

Among these five sample separation criteria, the results using group affiliation were most notable in that this hypothesis tended to be rejected for at least some of the parameters. We consistently found that the sensitivity of investment to cash flow was concentrated in the sub-sample of non-group-affiliated firms, with group firms showing little or no effects of cash flow on investment. The results for the Euler equation model were also consistent with this finding: the investment dynamics for group firms were consistent with the Euler equation specification in the absence of financial constraints, whilst the investment dynamics for non-group firms were not. The results from dividing the sample according to size tended to be consistent with these findings for group-affiliation. For all models, the sensitivity of investment to cash flow was stronger for smaller firms than for larger firms, and this effect was particularly significant for the Q model. For the other three sample separation criteria, these was less evidence of significant parameter instability.

From these econometric results, we can suggest three main conclusions.

First, by estimating the investment models using both the whole sample and the sub-samples, we can provide more direct evidence on the hypothesis of financial constraints. Blundell, Bond, Devereux and Schiantarelli (1992) and Hayashi and Inoue (1991) found financial effects on investment, but considered only full samples of UK and Japanese firms respectively (even if they used the Q model which is in theory a preferable model for investigating financial constraints, as Q should a sufficient statistic for expectational influences). Fazzari, Hubbard and Petersen (1988) offered a more direct test by dividing their total sample of US firms according to dividend payout behaviour. Devereux and Schiantarelli (1990) considered various sub-samples of their UK company data. Hoshi, Kashyap and Scharfstein (1991) also estimated an investment model using sub-samples of Japanese company data, divided according to whether the firm has a close relationship with a main bank or not. Our study provides a direct test of the hypothesis that financial constraints are more important for certain types of Korean manufacturing firms.

Second, we obtain consistent results across the four investment models. The coefficient on cash flow is positive and significant when using the whole sample; and coefficient differences are most pronounced between group and non-group firms, and to some extent between large and small firms, again over all four models. These results are consistent with the interpretation that financial constraints on investment result from a hierarchy of financial costs, and that the group-affiliated and large firms are less affected by this financial hierarchy. These differences between firms may reflect differences in the importance of asymmetric information or, in the Korean case, be the result of government intervention.

Third, the heterogeneous response of investment to cash flow, that we find in our study, indicates the importance of *heterogeneity* across firms. This is one of main reasons to conduct a microeconometric analysis rather than relying on a representative firm model and more aggregated data.

Two previous studies have investigated similar issues using company accounts data for Korea. Atiyas (1992) used data on 180 firms for 1984-1988, and a first-differenced GMM estimator similar to that used in our study. Dividing his sample by size, he found that financial variables were more significant in a dynamic Q specification for smaller firms in the period 1984-1986, although this was not the case for the later years 1987-1988. As we mentioned previously, these sub-periods are too short for reliable estimates to be obtained. When we divided our longer time period into the sub-periods 1982-1986 and 1987-1991 we did not find significant parameter instability over time, but this is clearly important issue for further research as more data becomes available.

Kong (1992) was closer to our study in that he focused on differences between Chaebol-affiliated and non-Chaebol-affiliated firms. However he used a Within Groups estimator and a static Q specification, neither of which was found to be appropriate for our sample. He also found stronger effects from cash flow for non-group firms for the early sub-period 1982-1985, but not for 1987-1989. As noted above we did not find such instability in our models. The present study extends this previous literature by considering a wider range of investment models and a data set covering both more companies and a longer time period.

Compared to previously published studies, our empirical results are most closely related to the study of Japanese firms by Hoshi, Kashyap and Scharfstein (1991). The main focus of their study was on the role of membership of a Keiretsu industrial group in reducing the impact of liquidity constraints on investment. As in our study, they divide their total sample into group-affiliated firms and non-group affiliated firms and postulate that these two sets of firms face information problems in the capital market in a different degree. They emphasize that the main bank at the core of Japanese industrial groups mitigates the importance of asymmetric information between lenders and borrowers.

Despite the similarity of the approach, it is important to stress that there are important differences between Japanese Keiretsu and Korean Chaebol. While Keiretsu were established rather artificially after the second World War around a main bank, which has an equity participation in each of the affiliated firms in a Keiretsu, Korean Chaebol do not have an in-house main bank.[10] For this reason, although testing for financial constraints on investment using sub-samples divided according to group-affiliation produced similar results for both Korea and Japan, our results for Korean firms should be interpreted in the Korean context.

As we argued in Chapter 2, it is expected that two forces in Korean corporate finance have served to relax the financial constraints on investment for some types of firms, especially group-affiliated firms and large firms.

First, government policy has systematically favoured Chaebol firms and large firms, sometimes directing banks to supply investment finance to these firms on more favourable terms than would otherwise have been the case. This practice is expected to have significantly reduced the difference in cost between internal and external sources of investment finance for group-affiliated and large firms, and may have increased this cost differential for non-group affiliated or smaller firms, as mentioned in Chapter 5.[11]

Second, in parallel with this government policy, the group-affiliated firms made efforts to create an 'internal' capital market to compensate for the absence of in-house banking. It was often the case that loans made to holding companies were diverted to other firms in the group, and group firms used such measures as reciprocal payment guarantees to facilitate external borrowing.

The above considerations have directly reduced the cost of external finance for group-affiliated and large firms. It is also possible that the membership of a Chaebol group enhances a firm's reputation as a borrower and reduces the importance of asymmetric information between lender and borrower. In sum, the factors that differentiate financial costs between group firms and non-group firms in Korea may work through government intervention, through direct benefits of group membership, or through an indirect signalling benefit. The econometric analysis reported in this chapter suggests that these factors have had a significant effect in reducing the impact of financial constraints on these firms' investment spending.

Table 6.1 Various estimates of the accelerator model: whole sample

Dependent variable: $\left(\frac{I_{it}}{K_{i,t-1}}\right)$

Sample period: 1984-91 367 companies 2534 observations

	(i) OLS	(ii) Within	(iii) GMM	(iv) GMM	(v) GMM
$\left(\frac{I_{i,t-1}}{K_{i,t-2}}\right)$	0.4139 (0.0250)	0.0673 (0.0293)	0.1386 (0.0608)	0.1510 (0.0566)	0.1520 (0.0561)
$\left(\frac{Y_{it}}{K_{i,t-1}}\right)$	0.0823 (0.0073)	0.0773 (0.0074)	0.0330 (0.0178)	0.0332 (0.0181)	0.0318 (0.0170)
$\left(\frac{Y_{i,t-1}}{K_{i,t-2}}\right)$	-0.0577 (0.0067)	0.0016 (0.0071)	0.0057 (0.0181)	-0.0045 (0.0165)	-0.0033 (0.0159)
$\left(\frac{CF_{it}}{K_{i,t-1}}\right)$				0.2660 (0.2026)	0.2991 (0.1335)
$\left(\frac{CF_{i,t-1}}{K_{i,t-2}}\right)$				0.0293 (0.1327)	
R^2	0.21				
m_1	-2.72	-9.35	-10.05	-10.18	-10.25
m_2	0.44	-1.10	0.04	-0.16	-0.17
z_1	378.51(3)	205.21(3)	41.52(3)	53.74(5)	53.78(4)
z_2	32.87(7)	69.56(7)	27.39(7)	25.56(7)	26.83(7)
Joint test (cash flow)				0.08	
Sargan p-value			58.24(47) 0.13	74.52(70) 0.33	75.21(71) 0.34

Notes to Table 6.1:

1) For the GMM estimator, the sample period is 1985-91 and the number of observations is 2167, as it uses the first difference of the equation.
2) Asymptotic standard errors are reported in parentheses. Standard errors and test statistics are asymptotically robust to general time-series and cross-section heteroskedasticity.
3) The m_1 statistic is a test for first-order serial correlation in the residuals, asymptotically distributed as standard normal under the null of no serial correlation. The m_2 statistic is a similar test for second-order serial correlation in the residuals. In all columns except column (i) these tests are applied to model residuals in first differences.
4) The z_1 statistic is a Wald test of joint significance of the reported coefficients, asymptotically distributed as $\chi^2(k)$ under the null of no relationship, where k is the number of coefficients tested. Degrees of freedom are reported in parentheses.
5) The z_2 statistic is a Wald test of the joint significance of the coefficients on the time dummies.
6) The joint test statistic is the p-value from a Wald test of the joint significance of the coefficients on the cash flow terms.
7) The Sargan statistic is a test of the over-identifying restrictions, asymptotically distributed as $\chi^2(k)$ under the null of instrument validity, where k is the number of over-identifying restrictions.
8) The instrument sets used are:

Column(iii): $\left(\frac{I_{it}}{K_{i,t-1}}\right)(t-2,t-6)$, $\left(\frac{Y_{it}}{K_{i,t-1}}\right)(t-2,t-6)$

Columns(iv-v): $\left(\frac{I_{it}}{K_{i,t-1}}\right)(t-2,t-6)$, $\left(\frac{Y_{it}}{K_{i,t-1}}\right)(t-2,t-6)$, $\left(\frac{CF_{it}}{K_{i,t-1}}\right)(t-2,t-6)$,

where the notation X(t-2,t-6) indicates that values of X from periods t-2, t-3, ... ,t-6 are included in the instrument set (where available).

Table 6.2 GMM estimates of the accelerator model: sub-samples

Dependent variable: $\left(\frac{I_{it}}{K_{i,t-1}}\right)$

Sample period: 1985-91 367 companies 2167 observations

	(i) Group	(ii) Size	(iii) Export	(iv) Age	(v) Industry
$\left(\frac{I_{i,t-1}}{K_{i,t-2}}\right)$	0.2322 (0.0824)	0.2229 (0.0601)	0.1261 (0.0765)	0.2315 (0.0697)	0.1295 (0.0627)
$\left(\frac{Y_{it}}{K_{i,t-1}}\right)$	0.0908 (0.0178)	0.0547 (0.0189)	0.0539 (0.0152)	0.0653 (0.0238)	0.0224 (0.0229)
$\left(\frac{Y_{i,t-1}}{K_{i,t-2}}\right)$	-0.0418 (0.0164)	-0.0094 (0.0152)	-0.0132 (0.0153)	-0.0266 (0.0176)	0.0669 (0.0182)
$\left(\frac{CF_{it}}{K_{i,t-1}}\right)$	-0.0821 (0.1880)	0.3111 (0.1726)	0.1220 (0.1299)	0.2423 (0.1311)	0.3719 (0.1349)
$D_i\left(\frac{I_{i,t-1}}{K_{i,t-2}}\right)$	-0.1524 (0.1054)	-0.1830 (0.0955)	0.0139 (0.1079)	-0.1310 (0.0975)	0.0331 (0.1171)
$D_i\left(\frac{Y_{it}}{K_{i,t-1}}\right)$	-0.0836 (0.0271)	-0.0554 (0.0322)	-0.0180 (0.0298)	-0.0138 (0.0295)	0.0410 (0.0368)
$D_i\left(\frac{Y_{i,t-1}}{K_{i,t-2}}\right)$	0.0628 (0.0262)	0.0269 (0.0282)	0.0142 (0.0298)	0.0199 (0.0266)	-0.0351 (0.0368)
$D_i\left(\frac{CF_{it}}{K_{i,t-1}}\right)$	0.5350 (0.2337)	0.1060 (0.2401)	0.0333 (0.1803)	-0.1120 (0.1701)	-0.1692 (0.2597)
m_1	-10.22	-10.11	-10.02	-10.41	-10.43
m_2	-0.77	-0.19	-0.27	-0.46	-0.38
Joint test (interactions)	0.02	0.10	0.80	0.09	0.70
Sargan	156.64	153.87	139.70	151.59	150.25
p-value	0.19	0.23	0.54	0.28	0.30

Notes to Table 6.2:

1) The dummy variable D_i which generates the interaction terms is defined by:

Column(i): $D_i = 0$ if the firm is affiliated to a Chaebol group
$D_i = 1$ otherwise

Column(ii): $D_i = 0$ if the average number of employees is over 1000
$D_i = 1$ otherwise

Column(iii): $D_i = 0$ if the ratio of exports to total sales is more than 30 %
$D_i = 1$ otherwise

Column(iv): $D_i = 0$ if the firm was established before 1960
$D_i = 1$ otherwise

Column(v): $D_i = 0$ if the firm is allocated to a heavy industry
$D_i = 1$ otherwise.

2) Except for the joint test, the test statistics reported are defined in the notes to Table 6.1. The number of over-identifying restrictions for the Sargan statistic is 142 for all columns.

3) The joint test statistic is the p-value from a Wald test of the joint significance of the coefficients on the interaction terms.

4) The instrument sets used in all columns are:

$$\left(\frac{I_{it}}{K_{i,t-1}}\right)(t\text{-}2,t\text{-}6),\quad \left(\frac{Y_{it}}{K_{i,t-1}}\right)(t\text{-}2,t\text{-}6),\quad \left(\frac{CF_{it}}{K_{i,t-1}}\right)(t\text{-}2,t\text{-}6),$$

$$D_i\left(\frac{I_{it}}{K_{i,t-1}}\right)(t\text{-}2,t\text{-}6),\quad D_i\left(\frac{Y_{it}}{K_{i,t-1}}\right)(t\text{-}2,t\text{-}6),\quad D_i\left(\frac{CF_{it}}{K_{i,t-1}}\right)(t\text{-}2,t\text{-}6).$$

Table 6.3 Various estimates of the error correction model: whole sample

Dependent variable: $\left(\frac{I_{it}}{K_{i,t-1}}\right)$

Sample period: 1984-91 367 companies 2534 observations

	(i) OLS	(ii) Within	(iii) GMM	(iv) GMM	(v) GMM
$\left(\frac{I_{i,t-1}}{K_{i,t-2}}\right)$	0.2441 (0.026)	0.0683 (0.0248)	0.1266 (0.0330)	0.1324 (0.0399)	0.1243 (0.0333)
Δy_{it}	0.3131 (0.0325)	0.3532 (0.0345)	0.2636 (0.1003)	0.2130 (0.1146)	0.2636 (0.1003)
$(k\text{-}y)_{i,t-1}$	-0.0719 (0.0091)	-0.3699 (0.0251)	-0.2261 (0.0420)	-0.1846 (0.0527)	-0.1823 (0.0531)
$\left(\frac{CF_{it}}{K_{i,t-1}}\right)$				0.2469 (0.1873)	0.2074 (0.1387)
$\left(\frac{CF_{i,t-1}}{K_{i,t-2}}\right)$				-0.0391 (0.1184)	
R^2	0.18				
m_1	-2.18	-8.81	-9.38	-9.58	-9.57
m_2	1.38	-0.80	-0.10	-0.17	-0.16
z_1	367.97(3)	249.37(3)	62.38(3)	73.93(5)	71.99(4)
z_2	35.22(7)	84.88(7)	36.95(7)	33.35(7)	33.10(7)
Joint test (cash flow)				0.31	
Sargan			100.17(80)	121.40(103)	121.73(104)
p-value			0.06	0.10	0.11

Notes to Table 6.3:

1) The test statistics reported are defined in the notes to Table 6.1.
2) For the GMM estimator, the sample period is 1985-91 and the number of observations are 2167 as it uses the first difference of the equation.
3) The joint test statistic is the p-value from a Wald test of the joint significance of the coefficients on the cash flow terms.
4) The instrument sets used are:

Column(iii): $\left(\frac{I_{it}}{K_{i,t-1}}\right)$(t-2,t-6), Δy_{it}(t-2,t-6), $(k\text{-}y)_{it}$(t-2,t-6)

Column(iv-v): $\left(\frac{I_{it}}{K_{i,t-1}}\right)$(t-2,t-6), Δy_{it}(t-2,t-6), $(k\text{-}y)_{it}$(t-2,t-6), $\left(\frac{CF_{it}}{K_{i,t-1}}\right)$(t-2,t-6).

Table 6.4 GMM estimates of the error correction model: sub-samples

Dependent variable: $\left(\frac{I_{it}}{K_{i,t-1}}\right)$

Sample period: 1985-91 367 companies 2167 observations

	(i) Group	(ii) Size	(iii) Export	(iv) Age	(v) Industry
$\left(\frac{I_{i,t-1}}{K_{i,t-2}}\right)$	0.0679 (0.0760)	0.1639 (0.0413)	0.0924 (0.0538)	0.1620 (0.0425)	0.1244 (0.0341)
Δy_{it}	0.3996 (0.1403)	0.4090 (0.1373)	0.2298 (0.1340)	0.4694 (0.1760)	0.2616 (0.1313)
$(k\text{-}y)_{i,t-1}$	-0.2367 (0.0764)	-0.2534 (0.0808)	-0.2193 (0.0899)	-0.2341 (0.0701)	-0.1622 (0.0670)
$\left(\frac{CF_{it}}{K_{i,t-1}}\right)$	-0.0497 (0.1847)	0.1128 (0.2023)	0.1964 (0.1710)	-0.0536 (0.1750)	0.2841 (0.1476)
$D_i\left(\frac{I_{i,t-1}}{K_{i,t-2}}\right)$	0.0502 (0.0839)	-0.1123 (0.0604)	0.0361 (0.0662)	-0.0795 (0.0684)	-0.0599 (0.0847)
$D_i\Delta y_{it}$	-0.1273 (0.1891)	-0.1169 (0.1915)	0.0759 (0.1869)	-0.2383 (0.2149)	0.1558 (0.2122)
$D_i(k\text{-}y)_{i,t-1}$	0.0372 (0.1034)	0.1324 (0.1077)	0.0350 (0.1104)	0.0545 (0.1002)	-0.1194 (0.1153)
$D_i\left(\frac{CF_{it}}{K_{i,t-1}}\right)$	0.4148 (0.2380)	0.2524 (0.2562)	0.0381 (0.2497)	0.3463 (0.2406)	-0.2695 (0.2536)
m_1	-9.526	-9.687	-9.531	-10.00	-9.801
m_2	-0.741	-0.738	-0.414	-0.548	-0.427
Joint test (inter-actions)	0.28	0.23	0.93	0.24	0.62
Sargan	142.66	157.03	157.92	147.95	148.78
p-value	0.52	0.22	0.20	0.39	0.38

Notes to Table 6.4:

1) The dummy variable D_i which generates the interaction terms is defined in the notes to Table 6.2.
2) Except for the joint test, the test statistics reported are defined in the notes to Table 6.1. The number of over-identifying restrictions for the Sargan statistic is 144 for all columns.
3) The joint test statistic is the p-value from a Wald test of the joint significance of the coefficients on the interaction terms.
4) The instrument sets used in all columns are:

$\left(\frac{I_{it}}{K_{i,t-1}}\right)$(t-2,t-4), Δy_{it}(t-2,t-4), $(k\text{-}y)_{it}$(t-2,t-4), $\left(\frac{CF_{it}}{K_{i,t-1}}\right)$(t-2,t-4),

$D_i\left(\frac{I_{it}}{K_{i,t-1}}\right)$(t-2,t-4), $D_i\Delta y_{it}$(t-2,t-4), $D_i(k\text{-}y)_{it}$(t-2,t-4),

$D_i\left(\frac{CF_{it}}{K_{i,t-1}}\right)$(t-2,t-4).

Table 6.5 Various estimates of the Euler equation model: whole sample

Dependent variable: $(I/K)_{it}$
Sample period: 1983-91   367 companies   2901 observations

	(i) OLS	(ii) Within	(iii) GMM	(iv) GMM
$(I/K)_{i,t-1}$	0.4066	0.1570	0.2618	-0.0700
	(0.0533)	(0.0532)	(0.0592)	(0.1718)
$(I/K)^2_{i,t-1}$	-0.2062	-0.0852	-0.1645	-0.1455
	(0.1087)	(0.1183)	(0.1360)	(0.3205)
$(\Pi/K)_{i,t-1}$	0.1087	0.0775	0.0581	0.0511
	(0.0149)	(0.0233)	(0.0322)	(0.0603)
$(Y/K)_{i,t-1}$	0.0050	0.0345	0.0230	0.0221
	(0.0020)	(0.0042)	(0.0055)	(0.0093)
R^2	0.19			
m_1	-0.39	-11.00	-11.52	-2.90
m_2	2.44	-1.80	-0.77	-3.39
z_1	433.78(4)	178.78(4)	89.94(4)	19.54(4)
z_2	29.41(8)	55.56(8)	37.79(8)	24.27(8)
Sargan			144.39(116)	91.10(84)
p-value			0.04	0.28

Notes to Table 6.5:

1) For the GMM estimators, the sample period is 1984-1991 and the number of observations is 2534.
2) The test statistics reported are defined in the notes to Table 6.1.
3) The instrument sets used are:

Column(iii): I/K(t-2,t-6), $(I/K)^2$(t-2,t-6), Π/K(t-2,t-6), Y/K(t-2,t-6)
Column(iv): I/K(t-3,t-6), $(I/K)^2$(t-3,t-6), Π/K(t-3,t-6), Y/K(t-3,t-6).

Table 6.6 GMM estimates of the Euler equation model: sub-samples

Dependent variable: $(I/K)_{it}$
Sample period: 1984-91 367 companies 2534 observations

	(i) Group	(ii) Size	(iii) Export	(iv) Age	(v) Industry
$(I/K)_{i,t-1}$	0.7989 (0.2319)	0.1239 (0.2252)	-0.1724 (0.1697)	-0.0197 (0.0728)	-0.1594 (0.1604)
$(I/K)^2_{i,t-1}$	-1.6968 (0.4207)	-0.2559 (0.3785)	0.0321 (0.2836)	0.0234 (0.1566)	0.2361 (0.3048)
$(\Pi/K)_{i,t-1}$	0.0346 (0.1129)	-0.0477 (0.0835)	0.0643 (0.0704)	-0.0387 (0.0442)	0.0457 (0.0682)
$(Y/K)_{i,t-1}$	0.0206 (0.0190)	0.0422 (0.0109)	0.0231 (0.0116)	0.0231 (0.0111)	0.0239 (0.0123)
$D_i(I/K)_{i,t-1}$	-1.1496 (0.2687)	-0.4329 (0.3054)	0.2168 (0.2969)	0.8876 (0.0556)	0.0738 (0.2304)
$D_i(I/K)^2_{i,t-1}$	2.0856 (0.4897)	0.6177 (0.5296)	-0.3014 (0.5116)	0.0387 (0.0946)	-0.6299 (0.4473)
$D_i(\Pi/K)_{i,t-1}$	0.0424 (0.1297)	0.1562 (0.1073)	-0.0519 (0.0995)	0.0281 (0.0404)	-0.0303 (0.1082)
$D_i(Y/K)_{i,t-1}$	-0.0015 (0.0219)	-0.0295 (0.0161)	0.0026 (0.0164)	-0.0196 (0.0094)	-0.0037 (0.0177)
m_1	-4.01	-4.39	-4.10	-5.66	-3.81
m_2	-4.20	-3.60	-3.72	-5.21	-4.01
Joint test (inter-actions)	0.00	0.18	0.92	0.00	0.48
Sargan	172.54	180.14	171.71	145.43	168.18
p-value	0.39	0.25	0.41	0.90	0.44

Notes to Table 6.6:

1) The dummy variable D_i which generates the interaction terms is defined in the notes to Table 6.2.
2) Except for the joint test, the test statistics reported are defined in the notes to Table 6.1. The number of over-identifying restrictions for the Sargan statistic is 168 for all columns.
3) The joint test statistic is the p-value from a Wald test of the joint significance of the coefficients on the interaction terms.
4) The instrument sets used in all columns are:

$I/K(t-3,t-6)$, $(I/K)^2(t-3,t-6)$, $\Pi/K(t-3,t-6)$, $Y/K(t-3,t-6)$, $D_i(I/K)(t-3,t-6)$, $D_i(I/K)^2(t-3,t-6)$, $D_i(\Pi/K)(t-3,t-6)$, $D_i(Y/K)(t-3,t-6)$.

Table 6.7 Static specification of the Q model: whole sample

Dependent variable: $(I/K)_{it}$

Sample period: 1983-91 196 companies 1666 observations

	(i) OLS	(ii) Within	(iii) GMM
Q_{it}	0.0083 (0.0042)	0.0112 (0.0047)	0.0023 (0.0136)
R^2	0.02		
m_1	7.83	-5.03	-6.18
m_2	4.51	-2.70	-2.29
z_1	3.80(1)	23.26(3)	36.23(3)
z_2	37.93(8)	24.88(7)	9.46(7)
Sargan p-value			56.44(33) 0.01

Notes to Table 6.7:

1) The test statistics reported are defined in the notes to Table 6.1.
2) For the GMM estimator, the sample period is 1984-91 and the number of observations is 1470.
3) The instrument set used in column (iii) is:
I/K(t-2,t-7), Q(t-2,t-7).

Table 6.8 Dynamic specification of the Q model: whole sample

Dependent variable: $(I/K)_{it}$

Sample period: 1984-91 196 companies 1470 observations

	(i) OLS	(ii) Within	(iii) GMM	(iv) GMM
Q_{it}	0.0089	0.0150	0.0007	0.0130
	(0.0054)	(0.0055)	(0.0121)	(0.0057)
$Q_{i,t-1}$	-0.0051	-0.0121	-0.0030	-0.0088
	(0.0056)	(0.0063)	(0.0177)	(0.0063)
$(I/K)_{i,t-1}$	0.3742	0.1185	0.2381	0.1999
	(0.0330)	(0.0315)	(0.0414)	(0.0382)
R^2	0.16			
m_1	-2.83	-7.10	-6.98	-6.83
m_2	0.61	-1.30	-0.57	-0.68
z_1	130.71(3)	23.26(3)	36.26(3)	33.99(3)
z_2	30.52(7)	24.88(7)	9.46(7)	28.30(7)
Joint test (Q terms)	0.19	0.02	0.99	0.07
Sargan			54.11(51)	99.67(80)
p-value			0.36	0.07

Notes to Table 6.8:

1) Except for the joint test, the test statistics reported are defined in the notes to Table 6.1.
2) For the GMM estimators, the sample period is 1985-91 and the number of observations is 1274.
3) The joint test statistic is the p-value from a Wald test of the joint significance of the coefficients on the current and lagged Q terms.
4) The instrument sets used are: Column(iii): I/K(t-2,t-7), Q(t-2,t-7) Column(iv): I/K(t-2,t-7), Q(t+3,t-7).

Table 6.9 GMM estimates of the Q model: whole sample

Dependent variable: $(I/K)_{it}$

Sample period: 1985-91 196 companies 1274 observations

	(i)	(ii)	(iii)
Q_{it}	0.0007 (0.0121)	0.0053 (0.0092)	-0.0031 (0.0086)
$Q_{i,t-1}$	-0.0030 (0.0177)	-0.0038 (0.0135)	0.0013 (0.0114)
$(I/K)_{i,t-1}$	0.2381 (0.0414)	0.2112 (0.0393)	0.1784 (0.0364)
$(CF/K)_{i,t-1}$		0.2082 (0.0809)	0.1677 (0.0621)
$(Y/K)_{i,t}$			-0.0679 (0.0174)
$(Y/K)_{i,t-1}$			0.0755 (0.0172)
m_1	-6.98	-7.15	-6.94
m_2	-0.57	-0.86	-1.97
z_1	36.23(3)	59.67(4)	76.23(6)
z_2	9.46(7)	12.81(7)	25.02(7)
Joint test (Q terms)	0.99	0.83	0.94
Joint test (output terms)			0.00
Sargan	54.11(51)	84.81(77)	127.46(102)
p-value	0.36	0.25	0.05

Notes to Table 6.9:

1) The test statistics reported are defined in the notes to Table 6.1.

2) The instrument sets used are:

Column(i): I/K(t-2,t-7), Q(t-2,t-7)

Column(ii): I/K(t-2,t-7), Q(t-2,t-7), CF/K(t-2,t-7)

Column (iii): I/K(t-2,t-7), Q(t-2,t-7), CF/K(t-2,t-7), Y/K(t-2,t-7)

Table 6.10 GMM estimates of the Q model: sub-samples

Dependent variable: $(I/K)_{it}$

Sample period: 1985-91 196 firms 1274 observations

	(i) Group	(ii) Size	(iii) Export	(iv) Age	(v) Industry
Q_{it}	0.0030 (0.0199)	-0.0052 (0.0115)	-0.0159 (0.0195)	-0.0186 (0.0228)	0.0124 (0.0159)
$Q_{i,t-1}$	0.0191 (0.0120)	-0.0018 (0.0159)	0.0269 (0.0208)	-0.0260 (0.0184)	-0.0027 (0.0174)
$(I/K)_{i,t-1}$	0.2491 (0.0621)	0.1959 (0.0493)	0.2820 (0.0671)	0.2309 (0.0511)	0.2043 (0.0494)
$(CF/K)_{i,t-1}$	0.0130 (0.1560)	0.1096 (0.1017)	0.1002 (0.0790)	0.2113 (0.1325)	0.2202 (0.0870)
D_iQ_{it}	0.0100 (0.0234)	0.0349 (0.0176)	0.0246 (0.0258)	0.0353 (0.0266)	-0.0073 (0.0206)
$D_iQ_{i,t-1}$	-0.0354 (0.0264)	-0.0360 (0.0229)	-0.0654 (0.0654)	0.0193 (0.0269)	-0.0228 (0.0283)
$D_i(I/K)_{i,t-1}$	-0.0616 (0.0790)	0.0081 (0.0794)	-0.0786 (0.0808)	-0.0099 (0.0787)	-0.0203 (0.0791)
$D_i(CF/K)_{i,t-1}$	0.2400 (0.1865)	0.2865 (0.1235)	0.1675 (0.1333)	0.1137 (0.1690)	-0.0510 (0.2010)
m_1	-7.12	-7.11	-7.33	-6.99	-7.36
m_2	-1.01	-0.68	-0.32	-0.50	-0.81
Joint test (inter-actions)	0.54	0.02	0.24	0.38	0.65
Sargan p-value	108.39 0.34	115.76 0.13	115.37 0.14	101.63 0.44	92.62 0.69

Notes to Table 6.10:

1) The dummy variable D_i which generates the interaction terms is defined in the notes to Table 6.2.
2) Except for the joint test, the test statistics reported are defined in the notes to Table 6.1. The number of over-identifying restrictions for the Sargan statistic is 144 for all columns.
3) The joint test statistic is the p-value from a Wald test of the joint significance of the coefficients on the interaction terms.
4) The instrument sets used in all columns are:
   I/K(t-2,t-4), Q(t-2,t-4), (CF/K)(t-2,t-4),
   D_i(I/K)(t-2,t-4), D_iQ(t-2,t-4), D_i(CF/K)(t-2,t-4).

Appendix 6.1: Data appendix

Sample

This appendix describes the calculation and sources of the main variables used in Chapter 6. It also presents some descriptive statistics for these variables. The accounts data was obtained from Korea Investors Service (KIS). Our sample consists of an unbalanced panel of 455 Korean manufacturing firms, which have at least 3 annual observations.[12] These companies were allocated to 9 industry groups by main products according to the Korean Standard Industrial Code (KSIC) as follows:

Group	Industry	KSIC code	Number
1	Food and beverage	31	42
2	Textile, wearing apparel and leather	32	66
3	Wood and furniture	33	7
4	Paper, printing and publishing	34	26
5	Chemical, petroleum, coal and plastics	35	111
6	Non-metallic mineral products	36	21
7	Basic metal	37	36
8	Fabricated metal products	38	138
9	Other manufacturing	39	8

The structure of the total sample is:

Number of annual obs	3	4	5	6	7	8	9	10
Number of companies	18	23	47	38	52	29	36	212

The structure of the sub-sample used for the Q model is:

Number of annual obs	3	4	5	6	7	8	9
Number of companies	56	37	16	18	16	12	150

First, we focus on the construction of our current-cost capital stock and tax-adjusted Q measures, and then describe the other variables used in the investment models of this chapter.

Calculation of the current-cost capital stock

In Korea, as in most other countries, accounting rules do not require replacement cost valuations to be reported. Gross fixed assets in the balance sheet is sub-divided into seven categories: land, buildings and structures, machinery, vehicles, tools and equipment, construction in progress and other fixed assets. However, we did not directly make use of this separate asset information in calculating our measure of the capital stock.[13] First, the investment figures for each individual asset were not consistent. For many companies there were some years in which all investment was classed as 'other fixed asset', and other years in which this was disaggregated into separate asset types. As a result of this, we considered the total investment figure to be more reliable. Therefore, we used the total fixed assets data and the total investment figure to calculate the current-cost capital stock.

We used a perpetual inventory method to estimate the current-cost capital stock. The replacement cost of the capital stock is calculated from the perpetual inventory formula

$$P^I_{t+1}K_{t+1} = (P^I_tK_t(P^I_{t+1}/P^I_t) + P^I_{t+1}I_{t+1})(1\text{-}\delta) \qquad \text{(A.1)}$$

where $P^I_{t+1}I_{t+1}$ is the increase of total tangible fixed assets minus the disposal of total tangible fixed assets and $P^I_{t+1}K_{t+1}$ is the replacement cost value of tangible fixed assets. P^I_t is the price of investment goods and δ is the rate of depreciation. The assumption here is that depreciation occurs at the end of the period (see Hoshi and Kashyap 1990), which is the usual practice in Korean accounts.

In our data, the year when balance sheet assets had last been revalued was available for each firm, and we used this as the benchmark year for our perpetual inventory calculation. In the year when the firm had its most recent asset revaluation, the replacement cost measure was set equal to the book value, and we calculated the capital stock for both earlier and later years from the perpetual inventory formula (A.1). The information on the most recent revaluation year was obtained from the 'Handbook of Korean listed companies' published by Daewoo Securities Ltd. In a very small number of cases the latest revaluation recorded was earlier than the start of our data for that firm. In these cases a benchmark based on the first year of net book value data was used.

Physical depreciation rate (δ): Our method of calculating depreciation rates for each firm takes advantage of the fact that book value data was available for seven separate categories of tangible fixed assets. First, for each firm, we calculated the weight of each asset type in total tangible fixed assets. We then computed a depreciation rate for each firm by taking a weighted average of separate depreciation rates for each of these assets. Rates for each asset were obtained from Hulten and Wykoff (1979,1981).

The depreciable assets (depreciation rate) were buildings and structure (5.17%), machinery (9.48%), vehicles (14.70%), tools and equipment (8.83%) and other fixed assets (5.74%). For both land and construction in progress, the depreciation rate was assumed to be zero.[14]

For each firm i and asset k, the weight is calculated as

$$w_{ik} = \frac{\sum_{t=1}^{T} AST_{it}}{\sum_{t=1}^{T} BTA_{it}} \tag{A.2}$$

where BTA_{it} is the total net book value of tangible fixed assets for firm i in year t and AST_{it} is the net book value of asset k. Using these weights, the depreciation rate is then

$$\delta_i = \sum_{k=1}^{7} w_{ik} \varphi_k \qquad \text{(A.3)}$$

where φ_k is the depreciation rate for asset k proposed by Hulten and Wykoff (1979). Although the net book value of each asset does not exactly reflect the proportion in which the assets are employed, in this way we are able to obtain firm-specific depreciation rates which approximately reflect the composition of each firm's capital stock.

Prices indices (P, P^I): For the output price (P), the wholesale price index (WPI) for all industry was used, as quarterly data for manufacturing industries was not available. An annual inflation rate for the firm's accounting year was estimated using the nearest four-quarter period.

The wholesale price index for investment goods was used for the price for capital goods except land and buildings. We also used the land price index for seven major cities. As most of the buildings and land for factories are situated in major cities and suburbs in Korea, this index is expected to be a good proxy. These price indice were obtained from the Bank of Korea Economic Statistics Yearbook and the Korean Development Institute Database. We constructed a weighted-average investment goods price, to reflect the division between land/buildings and other capital goods for each firm.

This price index was constructed as follows:

$$P^I = \alpha_{land} P_{land} + (1-\alpha_{land}) P_{other} \qquad \text{(A.4)}$$

where P_{land} is the land price index for seven major cities in Korea, α_{land} is the weight of land and buildings in the firm's total tangible fixed assets, and P_{other} is the wholesale price index for investment goods in Korea.

Constructing tax-adjusted Q

Following the formulation in Chapter 5, the tax-adjusted Q[15] can be characterized as follows:

$$Q_{it} = \left(\frac{V_{it} + B_{it} - A_{it} - TA_{it}}{(1-\delta)\ P^I_{it}\ K_{i,t-1}(1-\eta_{it})} - 1\right) \frac{P^I_{it}\ (1-\eta_{it})}{P_{it}(1-\tau_{it})} \qquad \text{(A.5)}$$

where V_{it} is the start of period stock market value of the firm, B_{it} is the start of period (book) value of net long-term debt, A_{it} is the start of period value of other net assets, δ is the depreciation rate, P and P^I are the price indices for output and investment goods respectively, τ is the statutory corporate income tax rate, η is the present value of current and future depreciation allowances for one unit of new investment, and TA is the present value of all current and future depreciation allowances that the firm can claim in respect of past investment, measured at the start of period t.

The detailed method of calculating each of these items was as follows.

Share valuation (V): The share price is the monthly average for the accounting month preceding the start of the accounting year, obtained from the Daewoo Securities Database. The share valuation is calculated by multiplying this average share price by the total number of shares outstanding at the beginning of the accounting year.

Debt (B): Book value of fixed liabilities at the end of the previous accounting year.

Other net assets (A): Book value of current assets (including inventories), investments and other financial assets, intangible assets and deferred assets, minus book value of current liabilities and deferred liabilities, all at the end of the previous accounting year. We make an adjustment to book valuation only for inventories. For Korean companies, inventory valuation can be categorised into three methods: 1)

FIFO method 2) LIFO method 3) total or moving average method. FIFO method does not require any inflation adjustment. LIFO method is affected by inflation, and we followed the standard adjustment method suggested by Salinger and Summers (1983) and Hayashi and Inoue (1991).

The adjusted value of inventories $P_t K_t^I$ is given according to the formula:

$$P_{t+1} K_{t+1}^I = \begin{cases} P_t K_t^I + (KB_{t+1} - KB_t)(P_t / P_{t+1}) & \text{if } KB_{t+1} \geq KB_t \\ P_t K_t^I + (KB_{t+1} - KB_t) & \text{if } KB_{t+1} < KB_t \end{cases} \tag{A.6}$$

where KB_t is the book value of inventories at the beginning of year t. The KIS data reported which method was used for different types of inventories.

Only about 4 % of the total sample used any method other than FIFO. There were some companies that used a mixture of these methods. If the part of inventories which used LIFO was not significant, or if it was difficult to judge the dominant inventory valuation method, we assumed that the firm used FIFO.

We used the same depreciation rate and price indices for each firm as detailed in calculating the current-cost capital stock.

Tax parameters Statutory corporate tax rate (τ): The rate of corporate income tax in Korea depends on whether the firm is listed and on the size of the firm. From 1982, the relevant corporate tax rate has not changed, and for a listed firm with a capital stock over 50 million won (which is clearly the case for most observations in our sample) the basic rate is 30 %. On top of that, the inhabitant tax and defence tax are levied at rates of 7.5 % and 2.5 % respectively (see Cho 1993, Kim 1991). The total corporate tax rate is therefore 39.3 %. We use this unitary rate throughout the period.

Depreciation allowances on a unit of current investment and past investments (η_{it} and TA_{it}): We assume that firms do not expect any changes in statutory tax rates and do not incorporate the investment tax credit into our calculation.[16] However, we do consider the special depreciation provisions in a simplified way. For the discount rate (r_t), we use the government bond rate.

The present discounted value of investment allowances on a unit of investment for each firm is

$$\eta_{it} = \tau_i \delta_i \sum_{j=0}^{\infty} \left[\frac{(1 - \delta_i^T)}{(1 + r_t)} \right]^j \tag{A.7}$$

where δ^T is the depreciation rate specified for tax purposes. Although Korean law does not require that commercial depreciation provisions are the same as tax depreciation provisions, this is the usual practice in Korea accounts, and we use our estimates of each firm's depreciation rate as a proxy for δ^T.

To calculate the value of allowances on past investment, we first calculate the stock of depreciable assets (K^T). Conceptually this can be represented by the relation

$$K_t^T = \sum_{s=0}^{\infty} (1 - \delta^T)^s I_{t-s} = (1 - \delta^T) K_{t-1}^T + I_t. \tag{A.8}$$

The stock of depreciable assets at the start of period t is then (K_t^T-I_t) and we estimated K_t^T using a perpetual inventory approach, based on equation (A.8) with the book value of the capital stock in the first period as the initial value.

The value of allowances on past investment that can be claimed in period t is:

$$CTA_t = \tau_i \delta_i^T (K_t^T - I_t) = \tau_i \delta_i^T (\sum_{s=0}^{\infty} (1 - \delta^T)^s I_{t-s} - I_t). \tag{A.9}$$

The present value of all current and future investment allowances on past investments (TA_{it}) for each firm can be obtained by summing discounted CTA_t into the future as follows:

$$TA_t = CTA_t \sum_{j=0}^{\infty} \left[\frac{(1 - \delta_i^T)}{(1 + r_t)} \right]^j . \qquad (A.10)$$

In Korea, in addition to this 'ordinary depreciation', special depreciation is granted to firms which fall into certain categories.[17] In our data, it is not possible to determine the extent to which firms have opted for pro rata special depreciation (in which case the effects of special depreciation extend into the future) or for lump-sum special depreciation (in which case the effect is limited to one period). From our data set, as only the total amount of special depreciation was available, we assumed that all these amounts were treated as a one-time lump-sum deduction, and therefore they affect the total depreciation allowance on a unit of investment for one time period as follows.

For each firm i,

$$\eta_t = \eta_t^0 + \left(\frac{SDEP_t}{ADD_t} \right) \tau_t \qquad (A.12)$$

where η_t^0 is calculated for ordinary depreciation, $SDEP_t$ is the special depreciation reported in year t and ADD_t is the increase in tangible fixed assets in year t.

Other variables

Investment (I): Investment is measured as the increase of total tangible fixed assets minus the disposal of total tangible fixed assets. These figures are both flows and taken from the financing table.

Sales (Y): Net sales.

Cash flow (CF): Net profit after interest, tax payments and preference dividends, plus depreciation provisions for tangible fixed assets.

Gross operating profit (Π): Operating profit before interest, tax payments and preference dividends, plus depreciation expenses for tangible fixed assets.

Descriptive statistics

Means (standard deviations) of the variables used in the regression analysis:

	Full sample	Group	Non-group
I_t/K_{t-1}	0.225 (0.205)	0.229 (0.194)	0.223 (0.212)
Y_t/K_{t-1}	3.458 (2.136)	2.752 (1.712)	3.871 (2.249)
CF_t/K_{t-1}	0.214 (0.158)	0.180 (0.131)	0.235 (0.169)
I_t/K_t	0.166 (0.124)	0.171 (0.119)	0.166 (0.135)
Y_t/K_t	2.994 (1.815)	2.373 (1.442)	3.353 (1.901)
Π_t/K_t	0.367 (0.223)	0.298 (0.158)	0.389 (0.247)
Q_t	-0.106 (1.188)	-0.127 (0.947)	-0.088 (1.352)

Deletion criteria

As in Chapter 4, if the firm has changed the month in which its accounting year ended, we retained the longest sequence of consecutive years in our sample. The full data set referred to in the table below is the result of this operation. In addition to this, we applied two further filters to obtain the data set used in the regression analysis of this chapter. First, we excluded observations where one of our measures of investment, capital stock, or sales increased or decreased by a factor of three or more from one year to the next. Second, we excluded very unlikely values of the variables used in the regressions, based on the empirical means and standard deviations of these variables in the full sample.

Whole sample		
	Number of firms	Number of observations
full data set	465 (448)	4260 (4166)
first filter	465 (430)	4086 (3930)
second filter	455 (367)	3649 (3268)
Q sample		
first filter	313 (199)	2208 (1796)
second filter	305 (196)	2062 (1666)

Note:

The figures in parenthesis are the number of companies and observations where six or more consecutive observations were available.

Specifically, if any variable of interest was more than three standard deviations away from its mean for the whole sample, this observation was excluded from the sample. After deleting observations according to each of these filters, we then retained the longest series of consecutive annual observations for each firm. The number of observations retained as a result of applying these criteria is reported in the table below.

Sampling criteria

1) Group affiliation: a firm is considered to be group-affiliated if it belongs to one of the 50 largest Chaebol groups (according to total group assets), and not group-affiliated otherwise.
2) Size: a firm is classified as large if the average number of full-time employees over the firm's sample period of each firm is over 1000, and considered to be small otherwise.
3) Export ratio: a firm is considered to be export-oriented if the ratio of total foreign sales to total sales is more than 30 %, and not export-oriented otherwise.
4) Age: a firm is classified as old if the firm was established before 1960, and considered to be young otherwise.
5) Industry: for the industries classified as heavy and light industries, see Appendix 3.1.

Number of firms for each sub-sample used

Whole sample (367 firms)					
	group	size	export	age	industry
$D_i = 0$	134	165	151	135	243
$D_i = 1$	233	202	216	232	124
Q sample (196 firms)					
$D_i = 0$	90	126	74	103	70
$D_i = 1$	106	70	122	93	126

Notes:

1) $D_i = 0$: group firms, large firms, export firms, old firms, heavy industry firms.

2) $D_i = 1$: non-group firms, small firms, domestic firms, young firms, light industry firms.

Notes

1. Industry classifications are provided by KIS and follow the Korean Standard Industry Code (KSIC).
2. The data on share prices and the number of shares outstanding were obtained from Daewoo Securities in Korea.
3. Strict exogeneity requires that x_{it} is uncorrelated with all past, present and future realisations of v_{is}. OLS would also be consistent in the static levels model if x_{it} were uncorrelated with α_i and only predetermined with respect to v_{it} (i.e. uncorrelated with current and future v_{is}, but possibly affected by past shocks), provided in this case that v_{it} is serially uncorrelated.
4. Group means are the mean of the observations for each individual. For time-invariant terms like α_i the group mean is simply α_i itself, so the transformation eliminates such terms from the model.
5. In practice time dummies can be included in the first-differenced equations to control for time-specific effects, since the number of time periods is small.
6. The instrument set includes values of $(I_{it}/K_{i,t-1})$ and $(Y_{it}/K_{i,t-1})$ for periods t-2, t-3,..., t-6 (where available). This allows the current sales term to be endogenous, as well as potentially correlated with the firm-specific effects.
7. In these columns, values of $\left(\frac{CF_{it}}{K_{i,t-1}}\right)$ for periods t-2, t-3,..., t-6 (where available) are added to the instrument set, allowing for possible correlation between $\left(\frac{CF_{it}}{K_{i,t-1}}\right)$ and v_{it}.
8. The indication of significant second-order serial correlation in the residuals in column (iv) does not contradict this, since instruments dated t-2 are not used in this instrument set.

9. We used these four models to assess the robustness of our results on financial effects to different model specifications. While with the accelerator and error correction models, we cannot simply identify the impact of additional financial variables, such as cash flow, with the presence of financial constraints on investment , the Q model and Euler equation model are more consistent with this interpretation, as discussed in Chapter 5.
10. For detail, see Cole and Park (1983) or Jones and Sakong (1980). Keiretsu were formed artificially after the Second World War since Zaibatsu, the earlier form of Keiretsu, were dismantled by force under US influence. Zaibatsu did not have a main bank and were controlled by the founder-family. It has been suggested that the present Korean Chaebol are more like Zaibatsu than Keiretsu (Jones and Sakong 1980).
11. It should be pointed out that this direct policy intervention declined during the 1980s, aided by the financial liberalization effort. We investigated the stability of our econometric models between the early and late 1980s, but did not find significant parameter differences. However, this may be due to the very small number of time periods available in our sample. The process of financial liberalization in Korea was also very gradual up to the end of the 1980s, and has been described by Amsden and Euh (1989) as a 'stop-go' process.
12. In the estimation, only the 367 companies with at least 6 observations were used.
13. We used the availability of separate fixed asset data in calculating the depreciation rate for each firm, as discussed below.
14. The weights using the total sample of firms were as follows: land (0.266), buildings and structures (0.292), machinery (0.267), vehicles (0.041), tools and equipment (0.054), construction in progress (0.071), and other assets (0.00).
15. Summers (1981) and Salinger and Summers (1983), using US aggregate and company accounts panel data respectively, concluded that the

tax-adjustment has a considerable effect on Q. Hayashi and Inoue (1991) reached the same conclusion.

16. According to Korean tax rules, the firm is entitled to an investment tax credit of 3 - 10 percent of the amount of investment if the investment is in any of the following business activities: 1) venture businesses using new technology; 2) businesses transferring their plant facilities to areas outside the large cities; 3) investments in energy-saving facilities; 4) purchase or construction of houses to be rented to employees; 5) investment in research and development and vocational training facilities. For more detail, see Cho (1993) and KPMG San Tong (1991). It was not possible to identify if firms were eligible for an investment tax credit in our data set.

17. There are broadly two kinds of special depreciation under the Corporation Tax Law and Tax Exemption and Reduction Control Law: 1) special depreciation equal to a certain percentage of the ordinary depreciation for such special investments as in machinery and equipment used for 12-13 hours per day or more and heavy equipment directly used in national land projects; 2) a once-and-for-all lump-sum deduction is available to firms investing in industries defined in the Industry Development Law. For more detail, see Cho (1993) and KPMG San Tong (1991).

7 Conclusion

In this book we have investigated the impact of financial factors on corporate investment in Korea using data for the period 1975-1991. Our main focus was on whether investment spending in the Korean manufacturing sector is constrained by the availability of finance, and whether some types of firms are more affected by financial constraints than others. For this purpose, we started with the discussion of the development of the Korean financial system and the Korean corporate sector, and of how the government's industrial policy in the last three decades has affected the financing of investment spending by Korean firms. We then analysed the actual patterns of investment finance using aggregate level flow of funds data and individual company accounts data in Chapters 3 and 4, respectively. Finally we used our sample of company accounts data to estimate a range of econometric models in order to investigate whether investment is affected by financial constraints and whether this is significant for firms with certain characteristics. We first summarise the main findings of each chapter and then conclude with some more general results of our research.

In Chapter 2, having summarised the effects of government intervention in the financial system, we argued that the discriminatory treatment of the corporate sector by the government prior to the introduction of financial liberalisation during the 1980s has resulted in a sustainable structure in which certain types of firms continue to enjoy favourable access to external finance compared to the other types of firms. We suggested that affiliation to a Chaebol group, firm size and export propensity, as well as age and industry classification (heavy/light industries) were likely to be important influences on a firm's access to external finance. These factors were therefore considered as sample separation criteria.

In Chapters 3 and 4, we investigated the pattern of investment finance in Korea, using flow of funds data at both the aggregate and the company level, respectively, following the methodology of Mayer (1988,1990) and Corbett and Jenkinson (1994). We found that the Korean corporate sector uses a relatively low share of internal finance and a relatively high share of loans in financing investment spending compared to other countries (US, UK, Japan and Germany). Using the company data, we observed some important differences in financing patterns between sub-samples divided according to the criteria mentioned above. In particular we found that Chaebol firms and larger firms tend to use significantly more long-term external finance and less internal finance, *pro rata*, than non-Chaebol firms and smaller firms; whilst differences in financing patterns among the other sub-samples were not as consistent as in the results from the group and size classifications. As we discussed in Chapter 5, this observation may be consistent with the suggestion that the investment spending of group-affiliated and larger firms is more likely to be affected by financial constraints than that of non-group and smaller firms. But since other explanations could also account for this pattern, we investigated the presence of financial constraints more directly through a rigorous microeconometric analysis of company investment data in Chapter 6.

In Chapter 6, we estimated a number of investment models surveyed in Chapter 5, to examine whether investment spending is affected by financial constraints, and whether such constraints are more important for some types of firms than others. We used four investment models, a sales-accelerator model, an error correction model, a Q model and an Euler equation model, to assess the robustness of our results on financial effects to different model specifications. Our empirical strategy was to estimate the investment models with cash flow as an additional explanatory variable - except for the Euler equation model which already includes a similar profits term - first for our total sample of companies, as in Blundell, Bond, Devereux and Schiantarelli (1992) for example; and then for sub-samples divided according to the above mentioned criteria to test for parameter constancy across these sub-samples, as in Devereux and Schiantarelli (1990) and Hoshi, Kashyap and Scharfstein (1991).

In the first stage, we generally found positive and significant coefficients on the cash flow terms, although the performance of our measure of Q was disappointing and the estimated coefficients in the Euler equation model were not satisfactory in the full sample. This sensitivity of investment to cash flow was further examined in the second stage of our analysis, dividing the total sample into various sub-samples described above. The results indicated that the investment spending of Chaebol group- affiliated firms is less sensitive to cash flow than that of non-group firms. We obtained some similar differences between larger and smaller firms, whilst the other sample separation criteria used did not reveal any significant parameter differences. These findings were generally robust across the range of investment models we considered. These results are consistent with the interpretation that the presence of financial constraints on investment results from a hierarchy of financial costs - with external finance being more costly than internal finance - and that the group-affiliated and larger firms in Korea are less affected by such a financial hierarchy.

Our results have some similarities to those of Hoshi, Kashyap and Scharfstein (1991), in that the firms that belong to larger industrial groups (the Chaebol in Korea and the Keiretsu in Japan) are found to be affected by financial constraints on investment. However the structure of these groups is quite different in Korea and Japan. In Japan the Keiretsu group has a main bank which has equity relationships with the member companies, which is not the case in Korea. In Korea, it is likely that the differences between group-affiliated and larger firms, and non-group and smaller firms may reflect differences in the importance of asymmetric information and/or the legacy of previous government intervention in the financial system and the allocation of investment finance.

The consistency between the differences in the patterns in investment finance between Chaebol-affiliated or larger firms and non-Chaebol firms or smaller firms that we found in Chapter 4, and the econometric differences in the sensitivity of investment to financial factors that we found in Chapter 6, emphasises the importance of heterogeneity within the Korean corporate sector. Although some previous studies (Atiyas 1992, Kong 1992) have investigated these issues in the context of a Q model of investment, we emphasize that our study has collected a larger data sample than has been used previously, applied more rigorous econometric methods, and obtained robust findings across a range of investment models.

Finally, it should be borne in mind that the accounts data used in this study were unconsolidated accounts data for individual corporations. Within a Chaebol group, funds may be directed from a company with high cash flow to a company with high investment demand. This leaves open the possibility that total investment spending may be constrained by total cash flow available at the level of the Chaebol group. This question could in principle be investigated using consolidated accounts data for Chaebol groups. It is also important to note that our sample period 1982-1991 was too short to seriously consider the effects of the financial liberalisation that occurred in Korea during the 1980s. These issues will be important questions for future research.

Bibliography

Abel, A.B. (1980), 'Empirical investment equation: an integrative framework', *Carnegie-Rochester Conference Series on Public Policy*, Vol. 12, 39-91.

Amsden, A.H. (1989), *Asia's Next Giant: South Korea and Late Industrialization*, Oxford: Oxford University Press.

Amsden, A.H. and Euh, Y.D (1993), 'South Korea's 1980s financial reforms: good-bye financial repression (maybe), hello new institutional restraints' *World Development*, Vol. 21, 379-390.

Anderson, T.W. and Hsiao, C. (1981), 'Formulation and estimation of dynamic models using panel data', *Journal of Econometrics*, Vol. 18, 47-82.

Aoki, M. (1984), *The Economics of Japanese Firms*, Amsterdam: North Holland.

Arellano, M. and Bond, S.R. (1988), 'Dynamic panel data estimation using DPD - a guide for users', Institute for Fiscal Studies Working paper, No. 88/15.

Arellano, M. and Bond, S.R. (1991), 'Some tests of specification for panel data: Monte Carlo evidence and an application to employment equations' *Review of Economic Studies*, Vol. 58, 277-297.

Atiyas, I. (1992), 'Financial reform and investment behavior in Korea', World Bank, mimeo.

Bank of Korea, (1990), *Financial System of Korea*, Seoul: Bank of Korea.

Bank of Korea, (various issues), *National Accounts*, Seoul: Bank of Korea.

Bank of Korea, (various issues), *Financial Statement Analysis*, Seoul: Bank of Korea.

Bean, C. (1981), 'An econometric model of manufacturing investment in the UK', *Economic Journal*, Vol. 91, 106-121.

Blundell, R.W. and Bond, S.R. (1995), 'The importance of initial conditions in dynamic panel data models', Institute for Fiscal Studies, mimeo.

Blundell, R.W., Bond, S.R, Devereux, M., and Schiantarelli, F (1992), 'Investment and Tobin's Q', *Journal of Econometrics*, Vol. 51,233-257.

Bond, S.R. and Meghir, C. (1994a), 'Dynamic investment models and the firm's financial policy', *Review of Economic Studies*, Vol.61,197-222.

Bond, S.R. and Meghir, C. (1994b), 'Financial constraints and company investment', *Fiscal Studies*, Vol. 15, No 2, 1-18.

Borio, C. (1990), 'Patterns of corporate finance', BIS Economic paper, No. 27, Bank of International Settlements, Basle.

Chen, S. and Chowdhury, G. (1992), 'Investment decisions in Taiwan and South Korea: Evidence from company accounts data', mimeo.

Cho, S.W. (1993), *The Korean Tax Law*, Seoul: Hyunam Sa (in Korean).

Cho, S. (1994), *The Dynamics of Korean Economic Development*, Washington: Institute of International Economies.

Cho, Y.J. (1989), 'Finance and Development: the Korean Approach', *Oxford Review of Economic Policy*, vol. 5, No. 4, 88-102.

Cho, Y.J. (1990), 'The financial policy and financial sector developments in Korea and Taiwan', in J.K. Kwon (ed.), *The Korean Economic Development*, Connecticut: Greenwood Press.

Cho, Y.J. and Cole, D. (1986), 'The role of the financial sector in Korea's structural adjustment', Development Discussion paper No. 2390, HIID, Harvard University.

Cho, Y.J. and Hellman, T. (1993), 'The government's role in Japanese and Korean credit markets: a new institutional economics perspective', PRE Working paper WPS 1190, The World Bank.

Choi, B.S. (1993), 'Financial policy and big business in Korea: the perils of financial regulation', in S. Haggard, C.H. Lee, and S. Maxfield (eds.), *The Politics of Finance in Developing Countries*, Ithaca: Cornell University Press.

Choi, D. and Cho, M. (1987), *Comparative Analysis on General Trading Companies in Korea*, Seoul: Korea Investors Service (in Korean).

Chowdhury, A. and Islam, I. (1993), *The Newly Industrialized Economies in East Asia*, London: Routledge.

Cobham, D. and Subramaniam, R. (1995), 'Corporate finance in developing countries: New evidence for India', Discussion Paper No. 9512, CRIEFF, University of St. Andrews.

Cole, D.C. and Park, Y.C. (1983), *Financial development in Korea 1945-1978* Cambridge, MA: Harvard University Press.

Corbett, J. and Jenkinson, T. (1994), 'The financing of industry, 1970-1989: an international comparison', CEPR Discussion Paper, No. 948.

Cummins, J.G., Harris, T.S., and Hassett, K.A. (1994), 'Accounting standards, information flow, and firm investment behaviour', NBER working paper, No. 4685.

Daewoo Securities (1992), *Handbook of Korean listed companies*, Seoul:Korea

Dailami, M. (1990), 'Financial policy and corporate investment in imperfect capital market', PRE Working paper, WPS 409, World Bank.

Devereux, M. and Schiantarelli, F. (1990), 'Investment, financial factors and cash flows: evidence from UK panel data', in R.G. Hubbard (ed.), *Asymmetric Information, Corporate Finance and Investment*, Chicago: University of Chicago Press.

Fazzari, S.M., Hubbard, R.G., and Petersen, B.C. (1988), 'Financing constraints and corporate investment', *Brookings Papers on Economic Activity*, Vol. 1, 141-195.

Gilchrist, S. (1989), 'An empirical analysis of corporate investment and financing hierarchies using firm level panel data', University of Wisconsin, mimeo.

Gould, J.P. (1968), 'Adjustment cost in the theory of investment of the firm', *Review of Economic Studies*, Vol. 35, 47-55.

Greenwald, B., Stiglitz, J., and Weiss, A. (1984), 'Informational imperfections and macroeconomic fluctuations' *American Economic Review*, 194-199.

Harris, J.R., Schiantarelli, F., and Siregar, M.G. (1992), 'How financial liberalization in Indonesia affected firm's capital structure and investment decisions', PRE Working Paper WPS 997, The World Bank.

Hayashi, F. (1982), 'Tobin's marginal Q and average Q: a neoclassical interpretation', *Econometrica*, Vol. 50, 213-224.

Hayashi, F. and Inoue, T. (1991), 'The relation between firm growth and Q with multiple capital goods: theory and evidence from Japanese panel data', *Econometrica*, Vol. 59, 731-753.

Holtz-Eakin, D., Newey, W., and Rosen, H.S. (1988), 'Estimating vector autoregressions with panel data', *Econometrica*, Vol. 56, 1371-1395.

Hoshi, T. and Kashyap, A.K. (1990), 'Evidence on Q and investment for Japanese firms', *Journal of The Japanese and International Economies*, Vol. 4, 371-400.

Hoshi, T., Kashyap, A., and Scharfstein, D. (1991), 'Corporate structure, liquidity and investment: evidence from Japanese industrial groups', *Quarterly Journal of Economics*, Vol. 59.

Hulten, C. and Wykoff, F. (1979), 'Economic depreciation of the U.S. capital stock', Report submitted to US department of Treasury, Office of tax analysis, Washington, D.C..

Hulten, C. and Wykoff, F. (1981), 'The measurement of economic depreciation', in C. Hulten (ed.), *Depreciation, Inflation and the Taxation of Income from Capital*, Washington: Urban Institute.

Jaramillo, F., Schiantarelli, F., and Weiss, A. (1993), 'Capital market imperfections before and after financial liberalisation', PRE Working Paper WPS 1091, World Bank.

Jones, L.P. and Sakong, I. (1980), *Government, Business, and Entrepreneurship in Economic Development: the Korean case*, Cambridge: Harvard University Press.

Keynes, J.M. (1936), *The General Theory of Employment, Interest, and Money*, London: Macmillan.

Kim, E.H. (1990), 'Financing Korean corporations: evidence and theory', in J.K. Kwon (ed.), *The Korean Economic Development*, Connecticut: Greenwood Press.

Kim, J.Y. (1991), 'A study on the cost of capital and effective corporate tax rates in Korea', KDI Policy Series, 91-32. (in Korean)

Kong, M. (1992), 'Tobin's Q, internal finance, and investment of Korean manufacturing firms: evidence from micro panel data', mimeo.

Korea Investors Service (1990), *The Report on Chaebol in Korea*, Seoul:Korea Investors Service.

Korea Investors Service (1992), *KIS line user's manual*, Seoul:Korea Investors Service.

KPMG San Tong (1990), *Accounting standards for business enterprises in Korea*, Seoul: KPMG San Tong & Co.

KPMG San Tong (1991), *Investment in Korea*, Seoul: KPMG San Tong & Co.

Lee, C.H. (1992), 'The government, financial system, and large private enterprise in the economic development of South Korea', *World Development*, vol. 20, 187-197.

Lee, D.H. (1988), 'The role of financial markets in Korea's economic development', KDI Working paper No. 8801.

Lee, Y.K. (1990), 'Conglomeration and business concentration in Korea', in J.K. Kwon (ed.), *The Korean Economic Development*, Connecticut: Greenwood Press.

Lucas, R.E. (1967), 'Adjustment cost and the theory of supply', *Journal of Political Economy*, Vol. 75, 321-334.

Mayer, C. (1988), 'New issues in corporate finance', *European Economic Review*, Vol. 32, 1167-1189.

Mayer, C. (1990), 'Financial systems, corporate finance, and economic development', in R.G. Hubbard (ed.), *Asymmetric Information, Corporate Finance and Investment*, Chicago: University of Chicago Press.

Mayer, C. and Alexander, I. (1990), 'Banks and securities markets: corporate financing in Germany and the UK', CEPR Discussion Paper No. 6.

Meyer, J.R. and Kuh, E. (1957), *The Investment Decision*, Cambridge: Harvard University Press.

Ministry of Finance, (various issues), *Fiscal and Financial Statistics*, Seoul: Ministry of Finance.

Modigliani, F. and Miller, M. (1958), 'The cost of capital corporation finance, and the theory of investment', *American Economic Review*, Vol. 48, 261-297.

Myers, S.C. and Majluf, N.S. (1984), 'Corporate financing and investment decisions when firms have information that investors do not have', *Journal of Financial Economics*, Vol. 13, 187-221.

Nam, S.O. (1988), *Financial Accounting*, Seoul: Ilshin Sa (in Korean).

Nam, S.W. (1992), 'Korea's financial reform: since the early 1980s', KDI WP No. 9207.

Nam, S.W. and Kim, D.W. (1995), 'The principal transaction bank system in Korea', in M. Aoki and H. Patrick (eds.), *The Japanese Main Bank System: Its Relevancy for Developing Countries and Transforming Economies*, New York: Oxford University Press.

Nickell, S. (1981), 'Biases in dynamic models with fixed effects', *Econometrica*, Vol. 49, 1417-1426.

Park, Y.C. (1994), 'Korea: development and structural change of the financial system', in H. Patrick and Y.C. Park (eds.), *The Financial Development of Japan, Korea and Taiwan: Growth, Repression and Liberalisation*, New York: Oxford University Press.

Prowse, S.D. (1990), 'Institutional investment patterns and corporate financial behavior in the United States and Japan', *Journal of Financial Economics*, Vol. 27, 43-66.

Salinger, M.A. and Summers, L.H. (1983), 'Tax reform and corporate investment: a microeconometric simulation study', in M.S. Feldstein (ed.), *Behavioural Simulation Methods in Tax Policy Analysis*, Chicago: University of Chicago Press.

Schaller, H. (1990), 'A re-examination of the Q Theory of investment using U.S. firm data', *Journal of Applied Econometrics*, Vol. 5, 309-325.

Schiantarelli, F. and Georgoutsos, D. (1990), 'Monopolistic competition and the Q theory of investment', *European Economic Review*, Vol. 34, 1061-1078.

Singh, A. and Hamid, J. (1992), 'Corporate financial structure in developing countries', IFC Technical Paper 1, International Finance Corporation.

Singh, A. (1995), 'Corporate financial patterns in industrializing economies: A comparative international study', IFC Technical Paper 2, International Finance Corporation.

Steers, R., Shin, Y. and Ungson, G. (1989), *The Chaebol: Korea's Industrial Might*, New York: Balliger.

Stiglitz, J. (1989), 'Financial market and development', *Oxford Review of Economic Policy*, vol. 5, No. 4, 55-68.

Stiglitz, J. and Weiss, A. (1981), 'Credit rationing in markets with imperfect information', *American Economic Review*, Vol. 71, 393-410.

Summers, L.H. (1981), 'Taxation and corporate investment: a Q-theoretic approach', *Brookings Papers on Economic Activity*, Vol. 1, 67-140.

Sussman, O. (1994), 'Investment and banking: some international comparisons', mimeo, University of Jerusalem.

Taylor, P.J. and Underwood, B. (1987), *Financial Accounting*, London: Heineman Professional.

Tobin, J. (1969), 'A general equilibrium approach to monetary theory', *Journal of Money Credit and Banking*, Vol. 1, 15-29.

Treadway, A. (1969), 'On rational entrepreneurial behaviour and the demand for investment', *Review of Economic Studies*, Vol. 36.

Wade, R. (1988), 'The role of government in overcoming market failure: Taiwan, Republic of Korea and Japan', in H. Hughes (ed.), *Achieving Industrialization in East Asia*, Cambridge: Cambridge University Press.

Wade, R. (1990), *Governing the Market: Economic Theory and the Role of the Government in East Asian Industrialization*, Princeton: Princeton University Press.

Whited, T.M. (1992), 'Debt, liquidity constraints, and corporate investment: evidence from panel data', *Journal of Finance*, Vol. XLVII, 1425-1460.

Williamson, O.E. (1975), 'Markets and Hierarchies: Analysis and Antitrust Implications', New York: The Free Press.

World Bank (1989), *World Development Report*, New York: Oxford University Press.

World Bank (1993), *The East Asian Miracle: Economic Growth and Public Policy*, New York: Oxford University Press.

Zysman, J. (1983), *Governments, Markets, and Growth: Financial Systems and the Politics of Industrial Change*, Ithaca: Cornell University Press.